Super Series
OPEN LEARNING FOR SUPERVISORY M

Principles and Practice of Supervision

No. 101

# ENRICHING WORK

Published
for
**The National Examinations Board for Supervisory Studies**
in conjunction with
**The Northern Regional Management Centre**

by
Pergamon Press
Oxford · New York · Toronto · Sydney · Frankfurt

| | |
|---|---|
| U.K. | Pergamon Press Ltd., Headington Hill Hall, Oxford OX3 0BW, England |
| U.S.A. | Pergamon Press Inc., Maxwell House, Fairview Park, Elmsford, New York 10523, U.S.A. |
| CANADA | Pergamon Press Canada Ltd., Suite 104, 150 Consumers Road, Willowdale, Ontario M2J 1P9, Canada |
| AUSTRALIA | Pergamon Press (Aust.) Pty. Ltd., P.O. Box 544, Potts Point, N.S.W. 2011, Australia |
| FEDERAL REPUBLIC OF GERMANY | Pergamon Press GmbH, Hammerweg 6, D-6242 Kronberg-Taunus, Federal Republic of Germany |

Crown Copyright © 1985. Published by permission of the controller of Her Majesty's Stationery Office.

*All Rights Reserved. No part of this publication may be reproduced, stored in a retrieval system or transmitted in any form or by any means: electronic, electrostatic, magnetic tape, mechanical, photocopying, recording or otherwise, without permission in writing from the publishers.*

First edition 1985

**British Library Cataloguing in Publication Data**

Enriching work.—(The Super series. Open learning for supervisory management)—(Principles and practice of supervision; no. 101)
1. Employee motivation
I. National Examinations Board for Supervisory Studies
II. Northern Regional Management Centre   III. Series
658.3′14   H5549.5

ISBN 0-08-033391-5

This work was produced under an Open Tech contract with the Manpower Services Commission. The views expressed are those of the authors and do not necessarily reflect those of the MSC or any Government Department or the Publisher.

Material Source: NRMC
Author: Richard Ellingham
Editor: Harry V. Pardue
Illustrations: NEBSS

Printed and bound by Avon Litho Limited, Stratford-upon-Avon, U.K.

# CONTENTS

| | Page |
|---|---|
| INTRODUCTION TO THE SUPER SERIES | v |
| STUDY NOTES | vii |
| UNIT OBJECTIVES | ix |

## PART A   MOTIVATION AND MOVEMENT

| | |
|---|---|
| 1. Introduction | 1 |
| 2. Motivation and Movement | 1 |
| 3. Movement: Assumptions About People at Work | 8 |
| 4. Limitations of Movement | 13 |
| 5. Summary | 16 |

## PART B   JOB SATISFACTION

| | |
|---|---|
| 1. Introduction | 17 |
| 2. Satisfaction at Work | 17 |
| 3. Summary | 31 |

## PART C   JOB ENRICHMENT

| | |
|---|---|
| 1. Introduction | 32 |
| 2. Job Enrichment | 32 |
| 3. Motivation: Alternative Assumptions | 35 |
| 4. Job Enrichment in Practice | 40 |
| 5. Job Enrichment | 44 |
| 6. Introducing Job Enrichment | 47 |
| 7. Job Enrichment and the Supervisor | 51 |
| 8. Summary | 56 |

## PART D   PERFORMANCE CHECKS

| | |
|---|---|
| 1. End Check | 57 |
| 2. Tutor Check | 59 |
| 3. Work-based Project | 60 |

## PART E   UNIT REVIEW

PART F    APPENDICES

1.  Extensions                                  64
2.  References                                  65


NEBSS RECOGNITION                               67
SUPPORT CENTRES                                 69
SUPER SERIES UNIT LIST                          70
NEBSS REGISTRATION FORM                         71
FREE CONSULTATION VOUCHER                       73

# INTRODUCTION TO THE SUPER SERIES

## OPEN LEARNING

The Super Series has been designed as a text-and-tape presentation for those who prefer self-study or who cannot attend courses on a regular basis.

As an open learning student, you have the opportunity of making a selection of units from our list to match your own requirements and you can study them when and where you wish.

## TUTORIAL SUPPORT

Each unit has been written in such a way that you can study on your own. Although the units are complete in themselves, in some cases they provide not only *knowledge* but the opportunity of developing *skills*. In order to gain these skills you will need to join with others working in small groups in a Support Centre, details of which are given at the end of this Unit.

These centres can also help with any queries that may arise from your study of the unit and offer facilities such as libraries, microcomputers and videos in addition to tutorial assistance both by telephone and in the Centre.

A voucher which entitles you to an initial FREE CONSULTATION with an Open Learning Tutor at a Support Centre is included with this unit.

# STUDY NOTES

INTRODUCTION

This Unit of Study, like all those in the 'Super Series' is specially designed for studying on your own. This means that you can work at your own pace, and where and when you like. If you have a query, need help or want to join a group in order to develop skills as well as knowledge, your nearest Support Centre can help you.

STUDY METHODS

*Where*. You can listen to the tape in the car or at home. You can read the workbook anywhere. But if you want to get the most from it you need to be able to concentrate without distractions like conversation, TV or children! You will also need somewhere to keep your workbook, papers and tape recorder together and in order.

*When*. This is entirely up to you. The writers who prepared the Units think that you will be able to complete them in about eight hours, though don't be dismayed if it takes longer than this as we all learn different things at different speeds. The best way, of course, is to plan in advance and to set aside a certain time on certain days in order to complete the Unit satisfactorily.

If the Unit forms a part of a training course, or you are working for a NEBSS Modular Award and want to join a group, you may need to take these into account when you decide on your timetable.

Perhaps the best advice is not to be too ambitious but start *regular* periods of study — say an hour at a time. This will yield far better results than occasional long periods.

*How*. Listen to the first side of the tape and then read the workbook, section by section.

This has Activities and Self-Checks and your success in these will indicate how well you are doing. If you find that you are not doing very well, go back over the text and try again. It may be that you were in too much of a hurry.

Make notes in the workbook, or in a file if you want to discuss them with a tutor, of key points, because actually writing them down is a very useful way of helping to memorise them. If you keep your tape recorder handy you can record ideas or queries as they occur to you.

References to books, videos and films are also made in this workbook for those who want to study in greater depth. The Support Centre or your local library will be able to supply copies.

CONCENTRATE ON WHAT YOU ARE STUDYING, READ AND LISTEN UNTIL YOU HAVE GRASPED THE MATTER NOT JUST FOR AN HOUR OR TWO BUT SO THAT IT REMAINS WITH YOU. And if you can discuss the facts and ideas with other people this will develop your understanding and help to retain them in your mind.

HELP!  Help is available from

- Yourself. Go back and try again. Don't give up. If you don't understand or sometimes find it hard going, go back to it at the beginning of your next study period.

- Your family or friends. Even if they don't understand the subject the act of discussing it sometimes clarifies the point in your mind.

- Your training staff at work.

- The Support Centre, by phone or a visit (but phone for an appointment on your first visit).

# UNIT OBJECTIVES

As supervisor, you are responsible for the output and productivity of your workteam. But, as you well know, this can be a heavy responsibility.

The purpose of this unit is to add to your knowledge of motivation and to help you to carry this responsibility with increased confidence.

This unit takes advantage of sound management theory — it is used here to provide valuable guidance and advice on the application of theory at your place of work. In short, studying this unit will assist you to create motivation.

**IN THIS UNIT WE WILL:**

- explore the traditional approach of using rewards and sanctions to influence work behaviour;

- identify causes of job satisfaction and examine the relationship of job satisfaction to productivity;

- consider how job enrichment can be applied in different situations and discuss its likely benefits to you;

- explore how a job enrichment programme may be introduced into any place of work.

AUDIO TAPE Side 1

Before you continue through the unit, you should now listen to Side 1 of the audio tape that accompanies this unit. You will find it useful if you refer to the unit objectives shown below whilst you listen to the tape. You may wish to make the objectives clearer to yourself by making a note or two on the page as you listen.

**OBJECTIVES**

When you have worked through this unit you will be BETTER ABLE to:

Distinguish between MOVEMENT and MOTIVATION and identify the way they are used to influence the behaviour of people at work.

Identify the causes of SATISFACTION and DISSATISFACTION at work and determine how a job may be changed to improve job satisfaction.

Devise and introduce job changes to ENRICH THE JOBS of the workteam.

# PART A  MOTIVATION AND MOVEMENT

## 1. Introduction

In part A we distinguish between movement and motivation as ways used to influence the behaviour of people at work.

Traditionally, managers and supervisors have relied upon rewards and punishments to move their people to achieve high productivity. However, more recently, supervisors and managers have found it helpful to adopt an alternative approach which we can distinguish as motivation.

## 2. Motivation and Movement

Dip into almost any book dealing with the job of a supervisory manager and you're likely to find references to the idea:

**ONE OF THEIR MAIN TASKS IS TO MOTIVATE THEIR WORKTEAM.**

Unfortunately, 'motivation' is one of those words that is frequently used but rarely defined. What might the word mean?

---

**ACTIVITY 1**   TIME GUIDE 5 MINUTES

Let's take a few moments to think about the meaning of the word MOTIVATION. Complete the following sentence with a few words of your own:

Motivation may be described as _____

_____

_____

_____

PART A

I'd complete the sentence as follows:

Motivation may be described as the process of getting a person to behave in a particular way.

OR

Motivation may be described as that which causes people to work enthusiastically and willingly.

REFERENCE 1
page 65

In the book "Modular Programme for Supervisory Development" motivation is defined as "creating a force or impulse that will move somebody towards a desired action or activity".

The definition seems to accept that one person is attempting to influence another's behaviour. It seems to follow from this:

**YOUR JOB INCLUDES INDUCING DESIRED BEHAVIOUR IN EACH MEMBER OF YOUR WORKTEAM.**

Your response to Activity 1 probably contained key words like:

**CREATING: INDUCING: BEHAVIOUR: FORCE: WILLINGNESS: PARTICULAR WAYS**

or similar such words.

## ACTIVITY 2    TIME GUIDE 10 MINUTES

List FOUR actual behaviours you would wish members of your workteam to adopt at work. For example, you might want them to 'KEEP COSTS DOWN'.

- _____
- _____
- _____
- _____

PART

Typical examples you might have used:

- To work to a high standard.
- To arrive at work on time.
- To maintain work quality.
- To be friendly towards colleagues.
- To follow company policy.
- To meet deadlines.
- To work safely.
- To exercise initiative.

I think we can usefully state the two basic ideas which have emerged so far:

**AS A SUPERVISOR, YOU ARE RESPONSIBLE FOR ENSURING THAT YOUR WORKTEAM WORKS EFFECTIVELY**

in order to ensure that their work is productive:

**THEY MUST WORK AND BEHAVE IN PARTICULAR WAYS.**

Let's now turn our attention to how you might influence the behaviour of your workteam.

EXTENSION 1
page 64

In a Video Cassette "Jumping for the Jelly Beans" the industrial psychologist FREDERICK HERZBERG said:

> "The surest way of getting someone to do something is to kick him in the pants — to give him what might be called KITA."

(KITA is less polite than Kick In The Pants!)

Herzberg went on to suggest that KITA may be applied in THREE ways:

FIRSTLY, to threaten or to use physical violence. Although unusual, it is 'accepted' practice in some situations. For example, the night club 'bouncer' may threaten violence to keep his customers in order. In some situations supervisors have been known to use a degree of violence or the threat of violence to control their people, particularly those of junior status such as apprentices.

The problem with this approach is that violence tends to breed violence. When people are kicked they are likely to kick back!

SECONDLY, instead of physical abuse, the supervisor may use verbal abuse. When a supervisor shouts at someone in front of their mates they attack the person's self image — psychological violence — making them look foolish and feel foolish. Like the FIRST approach this will also increase hostility between supervisors and their workteams.

THIRDLY, instead of relying on the 'STICK' of physical or psychological punishment, supervisors can use the 'CARROT' of rewards. According to Herzberg this involves rewarding people for required behaviour. A typical example is payment for overtime. Here the employer wants employees to work more productively and so might offer the carrot of extra reward by overtime payment. However people may come to expect the increased pay for overtime and press to have this built into their basic wage. In the long run, the use of such financial 'carrots' may mean providing ever more expensive rewards. This will lead to an increase in the cost of operations.

3

# SELF CHECK 1

TIME GUIDE 5 MINUTES

Describe, briefly, three ways that Herzberg claimed KITA could be applied.

• _____

_____

_____

• _____

_____

_____

• _____

_____

_____

## RESPONSE CHECKOUT

A supervisor might:

- Threaten or use physical violence e.g. against an apprentice for fooling about on dangerous machinery.

- Attack a person's self image e.g. shouting at them in front of workmates.

- Find a way of giving some extra specific reward for the behaviour wanted e.g. letting someone "slip off early" for getting a job done on time.

EXTENSION 1
page 64

As we've seen, it is possible to get people to do things by using the 'stick' or the 'carrot'. But, according to HERZBERG this is NOT motivation.

> If I kick someone they will move! And when I want them to move again, what must I do? I must kick them again! Similarly, I can charge a man's battery, and then recharge it, and recharge it again. But it is only when he has his own generator that we can talk about motivation. He then needs no outside help, he can do it himself.

This explains what Herzberg calls MOTIVATION by making a contrast with 'MOVEMENT'.

PART

Let's follow his argument:

It's possible to get people to MOVE (to do something) by using the 'stick' or the 'carrot', but each time you want them to MOVE you must use the 'stick' or the 'carrot' again. So;

**MOVEMENT IS CREATED BY SOME OUTSIDE STIMULUS OR FORCE.**

On the other hand he argues:

**MOTIVATION IS CREATED BY SOME INTERNAL STIMULUS OR FORCE**

where people are MOTIVATED to do something because they WANT TO DO IT.

Motivation then arises within a person — it begins in the mind. Therefore it does present some difficult problems to supervisors.

However this does not mean that we are powerless to induce motivation. It does mean that:

**MOTIVATION INVOLVES MUCH MORE THAN APPLYING THE STICK OR CARROT.**

## SELF CHECK 2 — TIME GUIDE 5 MINUTES

Respond by completing each sentence with a suitable word or words.

a) The cause of MOTIVATION lies _____ the individual.

b) Movement is caused by some _____ stimulus or force.

c) A supervisor can get people to MOVE by applying _____ .

d) People are motivated to do something when they _____ to do it.

### RESPONSE CHECKOUT

Typical words you might use are:

a) within; inside; internal to

b) outside; external; imposed

c) rewards; sanctions; 'sticks'; 'carrots'

d) want; desire; wish.

Other words with the same meaning are also suitable.

PART

We've now defined Herzberg's view of MOTIVATION by contrasting it to MOVEMENT.

> MOVEMENT is the process of influencing another's behaviour by applying some EXTERNAL force or stimulus.

> MOTIVATION is the process of influencing another's behaviour by creating or generating some force or stimulus WITHIN THE INDIVIDUAL.

Since your job as a supervisor includes influencing the behaviour of your workteam it seems that your job involves both MOVEMENT and MOTIVATION.

## ACTIVITY 3 — TIME GUIDE 5 MINUTES

Take a few moments to consider how you attempt to influence the behaviour of your workteam.

Write down THREE of the ways you have used in the past or might use in the future to get one of your workteam to do a slightly boring task.

- _____
- _____
- _____

A whole variety of means may be used — some more successful than others.

- PROMISING THEM FAVOURS
- REWARDING THEM
- THREATENING THEM
- MAKING THEIR WORK MORE INTERESTING
- REMINDING THEM OF THEIR DUTY
- SHOWING APPROVAL AND DISAPPROVAL
- FRIENDLY PERSUASION

PART

Many organisations set out to influence behaviour by means of movement rather than by motivation. This used to be an accepted approach to get people to do their work. In some organisations this may still be the case.

Before considering how we may use the motivation approach we need to look a little further into the 'movement' approach: getting people to move.

It's best not to get into arguments about the 'rights and wrongs' of this 'movement' approach, instead let's agree that it's useful to include it in our experience. However we should appreciate that:

**MOVEMENT WILL NOT BE EFFECTIVE FOR ALL PEOPLE IN ALL SITUATIONS.**

## SELF CHECK 3

TIME GUIDE 5 MINUTES

Respond to each statement by writing TRUE or FALSE in the space provided.

a) Supervisors can motivate their workteams by offering rewards for good behaviour and by using sanctions for poor behaviour.

_____

b) A supervisor should be concerned with BOTH the motivating and moving approaches.

_____

### RESPONSE CHECKOUT

a) False — Since both rewards and punishments are imposed from the 'outside' by management, they cannot lead to motivation. You'll probably recall that motivation is achieved by creating or generating some force or stimulus WITHIN the individual.

b) True — The job of supervisors includes influencing the behaviour of their workteams. They should therefore be concerned with BOTH moving and motivating their workteams. If the 'movement' approach — 'carrot and the stick' — works, supervisors might use it. But as this approach is limited then supervisors should also be familiar with the motivation approach — though this is the more complex approach.

# 3. Movement: Assumptions About People at Work

Certainly up to the first half of this century the most common method of influencing worker behaviour was through the use of externally imposed rewards and punishments — 'the carrot and the stick'.

REFERENCE 2  
page 65

In the book 'The Human Side of Enterprise' DOUGLAS McGREGOR claimed that this approach was based on certain assumptions that managers have about man at work. McGregor listed these assumptions under a heading THEORY X. The following three assumptions are drawn from this list:

- The average man at work has a natural dislike for work and will avoid it if he can.

- Because of their dislike of work, most people must be controlled and threatened with punishment to get them to work productively.

- The average man at work wishes to avoid responsibility, has relatively little ambition and wants security above all.

## ACTIVITY 4 — TIME GUIDE 8 MINUTES

Let's assume you believe that the people in your workteam fit the Theory X descriptions outlined above.

How would you get them to work productively for your section?

Jot down one or two ideas or methods.

_____

_____

Perhaps your response referred to the use of some external influences or force e.g. the use of rewards and punishments — the stick and carrot approach.

Assuming that man dislikes work, leads naturally to a second assumption — man at work must be subjected to external pressures and controls to get him to work at all.

PART

REFERENCE 2  McGREGOR puts it this way:
page 65

> "Because of man's dislike of work he must be coerced, controlled, directed or threatened with punishment to get him to put forth adequate effort toward the achievement of organisational objectives."

We are advised by McGREGOR to question our assumptions about people at work, because:

**THE ASSUMPTIONS WE HOLD ABOUT MEN AT WORK WILL AFFECT THE WAY WE SET ABOUT INFLUENCING THEIR BEHAVIOUR.**

By the way McGREGOR also developed an alternative view of man at work that he called THEORY Y. This alternative view is in stark contrast to the Theory X view and is dealt with a little later on in this Unit.

Now let's consider one of the most influential management theories that developed from the types of assumptions contained in McGregor's Theory X.

REFERENCE 3  This theory is known as 'Scientific Management' and was developed by FREDERICK WINSLOW TAYLOR early this century in the U.S.A.
page 65

EXTENSION 2  Writing then, TAYLOR was obsessed with the idea of increasing the efficiency of an organisation in order to maximise profits. He claimed to have identified three major obstacles to achievement of maximum profits:
page 64

- The commonly held belief among the workforce that increased productivity will lead to a loss of jobs and result in unemployment.

- The belief that the workforce will deliberately hold down their output, and thus their earnings, to discourage management from lowering wage rates.

- That a workforce usually adopts inefficient and rule-of-thumb methods which are then passed on to others in the workforce.

According to TAYLOR, job security and high wages could only come from the high profits arising from the application of scientific principles to the management of organisations. This scientific approach is based upon:

- A scientific study of work to find the most EFFICIENT METHOD OF DOING WORK.

- A scientific study of management to find the most EFFICIENT METHOD OF CONTROLLING THE WORKFORCE.

Many ideas of scientific management are still in use; they form the basis for Method Study, Work Study and Time Study which are currently in common use.

The application of scientific management has, over the years, led to the development of the production lines we see for car and TV assembly.

PART

# ACTIVITY 5

TIME GUIDE 8 MINUTES

Now let's consider the extent to which your workteam are CONTROLLED at work. Take a few moments and think about the work done by ONE of your workteam. Write their job title in the space provided.

JOB TITLE _____

Now answer the following questions by writing YES or NO in the space provided.

a) Can he control the pace at which he works?  _____

b) Can he determine the order or sequence in which he does the work?  _____

c) Can he decide how he does the work?  _____

d) Can he decide when he does the work?  _____

e) Can he choose the tools and equipment he uses to do the job?  _____

f) Can he influence the quality of the work he produces?  _____

g) Can he decide where he does the work?  _____

If you compare the number of NO responses to the number of YES responses you will get some idea of the extent to which he is controlled by others. The more NO responses, the greater the degree of external control.

Most workteams are subject to SOME external control, and many others are subject to a HIGH degree of external control.

PART

**REFERENCE 3**
**page 65**

According to F W TAYLOR, a HIGH DEGREE OF CONTROL is necessary in order to get employees to work efficiently.

In one of his most well known studies he applied his 'scientific principles' to the shovelling of coke for the blast furnaces at a steel plant. HE SPECIFIED EVERY ASPECT OF THE TASK — the size of the shovel, the bite into the pile, the weight of the scoop, the distance to walk, the arc of the swing and the frequency and duration of rest breaks.

The results were most impressive. The shovellers increased their output from twelve and half tons to forty seven tons shifted per day. For this improved productivity they received higher wages.

In order to encourage the workforce to accept highly controlled jobs, Taylor paid them relatively high wages. It was his belief that "what workmen want from their employers beyond anything else is high wages".

In an attempt to get men to work efficiently, Taylor relied on the techniques of 'movement' rather than those of 'motivation'. He used the 'carrot' of high wages and the 'stick' of disciplinary action.

Due to the successes of F W Taylor and the 'logic' of 'scientific management', many of his ideas can still be found in many organisations today. It's hardly surprising therefore that many managers and supervisors spend a great deal of time and energy trying to 'move' rather than to 'motivate' their workteams.

## SELF CHECK 4

TIME GUIDE 5 MINUTES

From the following list of assumptions that supervisors hold about their workteams, which THREE most closely fit McGREGOR'S Theory X view:

a) The average person dislikes work and will avoid it if he can.

b) The average person will exercise self-direction and self-control at work.

c) The average person seeks responsibility at work.

d) The average person prefers to be directed and told what to do at work.

e) The average person has to be coerced and threatened with punishment to encourage him to work.

f) The average person is capable of a relatively high degree of imagination, ingenuity and creativity in solving problems at work.

PART

### RESPONSE CHECKOUT

a), d) and e) — each fit McGregor's Theory X view.

You'll probably recall that under Theory X it is assumed that people at work have an inherent dislike for work and will avoid it if at all possible. Because of this he must be directed, coerced and punished in order to get him to work at all.

The other three assumptions b), c) and f) are based upon an entirely different view of people that McGregor called Theory Y. We will deal with this view a little later on in this Unit.

Now a question on two of the ideas of F W Taylor and his 'Scientific Management':

### SELF CHECK 5

TIME GUIDE 5 MINUTES

REFERENCE 4
page 65

Respond by completing each sentence with a suitable word or words.

a) Scientific Management sets out to discover the most _____ method of doing the job and also to establish the most effective methods of _____ workteams.

b) According to F W TAYLOR the most important thing people at work want from employers is _____ .

c) In his attempts to improve efficiency, Taylor tried to _____ rather than motivate his workforce.

### RESPONSE CHECKOUT

Typical words you might use are:

a) 1st word: efficient; effective; profitable
   2nd word: controlling; disciplining

b) high wages; money; top earnings

c) move

Other words with the same meaning are also suitable.

PART

# 4. Limitations of Movement

So far we've accepted that supervisors such as yourself may well spend a good deal of time and energy using external controls to influence the behaviour of their workforce. Now let's assess the success or otherwise of this approach in achieving high productivity.

## ACTIVITY 6 — TIME GUIDE 5 MINUTES

Think about the extent to which your workteam respond to external control.

Respond to this question by putting a tick against the ONE answer which is most correct.

How many in your workteam work to what you consider is an acceptable standard, only because of external control?

a) All of them.

b) Most of them.

c) About half of them.

d) Few of them.

e) None of them.

How does your workteam compare with those of your supervisory colleagues? Why not check out their responses to this same question.

---

It is likely that some people respond well to external control whilst others do not. This proportion will vary from one workplace to another. Let's have a brief look at some research carried out in the car industry.

I've chosen car production as the example because the job of the car assembly worker is very highly controlled. Each job must be completed as the car moves on the conveyor through each workplace. Men are not permitted to leave their work station without their supervisor's clear permission. Each job is also very simple to do.

REFERENCE 4
page 65

In a study of the manual workforce at Vauxhall Cars in Luton, GOLDTHORPE AND LOCKWOOD discovered that they mostly had an INSTRUMENTAL approach towards work. That is, they were prepared to work to standards set by management, on highly controlled, dissatisfying jobs in return for high wages. These high wages allowed for a high standard of living which they enjoyed. Thus the work was 'INSTRUMENTAL' in them attaining a high standard of living.

PART A

EXTENSION 3  
page 64

At about the same time as this Vauxhall study, VOLVO IN SWEDEN, were experiencing major problems with their car assembly plant. Absenteeism was running at 20 to 25 per cent and labour turnover exceeded 40 per cent per year. The point was made that absenteeism and turnover were so high that they cancelled out the advantages of assembly line production.

It seems clear then that a large number of the workforce were no longer prepared to work to the standards demanded by management in return for the high wages offered. As the costs of their absenteeism and turnover rose, Volvo's management were encouraged to develop alternative methods of making cars — methods that would lead to more interesting and satisfying jobs for their workforce. Returning to the terms we've used previously,

**THEY WERE ENCOURAGED TO CHANGE FROM TRYING TO 'MOVE' TO TRYING TO 'MOTIVATE' THEIR WORKFORCE.**

A number of important general points can be drawn from these researches into car assembly.

1. Some people at work are willing to accept dissatisfying jobs, and in return for external rewards (usually high pay) are quite prepared to work to the standards demanded by management.

2. Others will react adversely to highly controlled and dissatisfying jobs, by resorting to various forms of disruptive behaviour e.g. excessive grumbling, absenteeism, lateness, leaving the company etc.

3. When a high proportion of people at work resort to disruptive behaviours the costs of production are significantly increased.

4. When these costs reach an unacceptable level, management should be encouraged to seek alternative methods of influencing the behaviour of their people. They should be encouraged to change from trying to 'move', to trying to 'motivate' them.

For supervisors, the advice is:

> When too many of your workteam adopt disruptive behaviours as a reaction to the controls placed upon them, then:

**TRY TO CHANGE FROM 'MOVING' TO MOTIVATION**

**OR**

**TRY TO IMPROVE THE MOTIVATION YOU OFFER.**

In Part B we direct our attention to those things which can be done to improve Motivation.

PART

# SELF CHECK 6

TIME GUIDE 5 MINUTES

Respond to each statement by writing TRUE or FALSE in the space provided.

a) Many people at work adopt an 'instrumental' approach to work.

_____

b) External controls can be successful in getting people to work to the required standards.

_____

c) The way workers react to external controls can influence the costs of production.

_____

d) When 'movement' fails to achieve efficient production, the supervisor should try 'motivation'.

_____

---

### RESPONSE CHECKOUT

a) True  It is not possible to say with any certainty how many people exhibit an instrumental approach to work. As we saw in the car assembly examples, some people do whilst others do not. You should be aware of the approach that each of your workteam has to their work.

b) True  When people have an instrumental approach to work, external control can be effective in getting many of them to work at the required standards. However we need to watch out for signs of discontent — e.g. absenteeism, leaving etc.

c) True  As we saw at Volvo, when people react to highly controlled situations by being disruptive, this increases the costs of production.

d) True  'Movement' can lead to efficient production BUT IF IT FAILS, WE MUST THINK ABOUT WAYS OF INTRODUCING MOTIVATION.

PART A

# 5. Summary

In Part A we focused upon the distinctions between MOVEMENT and MOTIVATION.

Both are concerned with influencing the behaviour of others.

- MOVEMENT is achieved by the application of some external stimulus or force.

- MOTIVATION is created by a stimulus or force from within the individual.

Many managers and supervisors have ASSUMED that people have a natural dislike of work and will avoid it if at all possible. These and other SIMILAR ASSUMPTIONS have led management to rely upon a system of rewards and punishments to move their workforce in an attempt to achieve efficient production.

This 'stick and carrot' approach has been only PARTIALLY SUCCESSFUL. It works for some people in some situations, but NOT FOR ALL PEOPLE IN ALL SITUATIONS.

When MOVEMENT has not worked, supervisors and managers have found it useful to look to the alternative and provide MOTIVATION to achieve the desired results.

# PART B   JOB SATISFACTION

## 1. Introduction

In Part B we shall consider the causes of job satisfaction.

We shall also:

1   Identify and distinguish between the factors that cause SATISFACTION and those that cause DISSATISFACTION at work.

2   Examine the probable relationship between JOB SATISFACTION and PRODUCTIVITY.

## 2. Satisfaction at Work

Before we consider what others have to say on the subject, try to identify those things that lead you to be satisfied with your work and those that lead you to be dissatisfied with work.

### ACTIVITY 7   TIME GUIDE 10 MINUTES

List THREE things which cause you to be satisfied with your work and THREE things which cause you to be dissatisfied.

THREE things which cause me to be SATISFIED with my work are:

- _____
- _____
- _____

The THREE things that cause me to be dissatisfied with my work are:

- _____
- _____
- _____

Check your responses to these views of two supervisors who were asked the same questions, though they listed FIVE things:

### Supervisor — Arthur

*Things causing satisfaction*

- High wage.
- Interesting work.
- Pleasant working conditions.
- Helpful boss.
- Friendly workmates.

*Things causing dissatisfaction*

- Low pay.
- Boring work.
- Poor conditions.
- Unfriendly boss.
- No friends at work.

### Supervisor — Bill

*Things causing satisfaction*

- Interesting work.
- Seeing the job through to the end.
- Having control over what I do.
- Being responsible for others.
- Knowing when I do a good job.

*Things causing dissatisfaction*

- Poor pay.
- A boss who is always on my back.
- Petty company rules.
- Too much form filling.
- Poor working conditions.

Look at Arthur's list. The things that cause him satisfaction are the OPPOSITE to those that cause him dissatisfaction.

For example, HIGH WAGES lead to his satisfaction whilst LOW WAGES cause him dissatisfaction.

But for Bill, those items that cause him satisfaction are entirely DIFFERENT from those that cause him dissatisfaction.

For example, in Bill's list, INTERESTING WORK appears in his list of satisfiers, but UNINTERESTING WORK does not appear in his list of dissatisfiers. In other words, the things causing Bill dissatisfaction ARE NOT the opposite to those causing him satisfaction, they ARE QUITE DIFFERENT THINGS.

REFERENCE 5
page 65

PART B

A researcher, FREDERICK HERZBERG, asked 200 accountants and engineers to describe those times when they felt EXCEPTIONALLY GOOD about their jobs and those other times when they felt EXCEPTIONALLY BAD about them.

His analysis showed that for most people, what caused the good feelings were DIFFERENT to what caused the bad feelings. These results were repeated in further studies involving men and women from a variety of occupations in America and Europe.

These, and the findings from other similar studies led Herzberg to a significant conclusion about satisfaction at work.

**THE FACTORS PRODUCING JOB SATISFACTION ARE QUITE DIFFERENT FROM THE FACTORS THAT LEAD TO JOB DISSATISFACTION.**

Let's look again at this conclusion.

Wouldn't it be obvious to put JOB DISSATISFACTION as the opposite of JOB SATISFACTION?

If we flick back to Arthur's list we would say 'Yes' — however, looking at Bill's list we have to say 'No'.

For instance, for Arthur, pay can cause satisfaction or dissatisfaction, but for Bill pay can only cause dissatisfaction.

Hence, we are not simply playing with words,

**WE ARE MAKING IMPORTANT DISTINCTIONS BETWEEN THE THINGS WHICH CAN CAUSE SATISFACTION AND THOSE WHICH CAN CAUSE DISSATISFACTION AT WORK.**

Understanding these distinctions will help you to motivate your workteam.

## SELF CHECK 7   TIME GUIDE 5 MINUTES

a) Flick back to the opinions expressed by our supervisors, Arthur and Bill, on the causes of satisfaction and dissatisfaction at work.

Whose list most clearly supports the research findings of Herzberg? Arthur's or Bill's? _____

Respond to each statement by writing TRUE or FALSE in the space provided.

b) "Herzberg found that the opposite to Job Satisfaction was Job Dissatisfaction". _____

c) Herzberg found that if something could cause Job Satisfaction then its absence would cause Dissatisfaction. _____

PART B

> RESPONSE CHECKOUT
>
> a) Bill's opinions most clearly support the findings of Herzberg. You'll recall that Bill views the causes of satisfaction as DIFFERENT from the causes of dissatisfaction, whilst Arthur sees them as OPPOSITES.
>
> b) False: the opposite to Job Satisfaction according to Herzberg is No Job Satisfaction.
>
> c) False: the absence of something which can cause Job Satisfaction will prevent Job Satisfaction from occurring. It will not lead to Job Dissatisfaction.

The explanations for this Self Check are pretty difficult to grasp. This following section should make these issues clearer.

EXTENSION 1
page 64

## 2.1. Herzberg's Two-factor Theory

Since Herzberg identified ONE SET of factors that may satisfy and a SECOND SET of factors that may dissatisfy, his theory is referred to as his Two-Factor Theory.

When he compared the factors which can cause satisfaction with those which can cause dissatisfaction, Herzberg noticed an important difference between them. Let's see if you can discover this distinction for yourself.

HERZBERG'S TWO-FACTOR THEORY

THE WORK FACTORS WHICH CAN CAUSE SATISFACTION...

THE WORK FACTORS WHICH CAN CAUSE DISSATISFACTION...

WHAT THREE FACTORS DID YOU LIST IN ACTIVITY 7?

AND, AGAIN, WHAT DID YOU LIST?

SO — WHAT IS THE DISTINCTION, EH?

PART B

# ACTIVITY 8

TIME GUIDE 10 MINUTES

Let's have another look at our Supervisors' lists: look at Bill's views on the causes of his satisfaction and dissatisfaction at work.

a) Look first at his list of items causing Satisfaction — in what way are these the same? Write down a few words or ideas:

- Interesting work.
- Being responsible for others.
- Having control over what I do.
- Knowing when I do a good job.
- Seeing the job through to the end.

_____

_____

_____

b) Now look at his list of items causing Dissatisfaction — in what way are these things the same? Write down a few words or ideas:

- Poor pay.
- Too much form filling.
- Petty company rules.
- Poor working conditions.
- A boss who is always on his back.

_____

_____

_____

c) When you compare your two responses above in what way are they different? Write down a few words or ideas:

_____

_____

_____

I appreciate that these are difficult questions SO DON'T EXCEED MY TIME GUIDE — just turn the page and you will see what I am leading to.

PART

> Check out your responses and see if you can agree with these:
>
> a) The factors that cause Bill SATISFACTION seem to be:
>
> - directly located in the actual job being done;
>
> - rewards.
>
> Generally these are to do with INTERNAL personal feelings.
>
> b) The factors that cause Bill DISSATISFACTION seem to be:
>
> - located in the Company and somewhat isolated from the actual job;
>
> - sanctions.
>
> Generally these are to do with EXTERNAL conditions.
>
> c) For Bill the differences are whether the factor is:
>
> - under his control OR controlled by others in the organisation;
>
> - in his actual work OR in the Organisation Policy and Procedures;
>
> - Reward OR Sanction.

This was not an easy Activity — it was intended to provoke thought and prepare us for getting to grips with HERZBERG'S TWO-FACTOR THEORY.

According to Herzberg, TWO important conclusions arise from his researches:

- The causes of satisfaction at work lie in the CONTENT of the job itself.

- The causes of dissatisfaction lie in the WORKING ENVIRONMENT.

Therefore:

**THE FACTORS CONCERNED WITH THE CONTENT OF THE JOB CAN CREATE MOTIVATION AND HE CALLED THEM THE MOTIVATORS.**

**THE FACTORS CONCERNED WITH THE WORKING ENVIRONMENT CANNOT CREATE MOTIVATION AND HE CALLED THEM THE HYGIENE FACTORS.**

The use of the term HYGIENE, ('borrowed' from Biology), Herzberg found useful. He claimed that poor hygiene meant germs and bacteria which could infect a person and cause illness. Good hygiene, however, would not cause fitness and muscular development — for these purposes other things like, nutrition and exercise, were needed.

So HYGIENE factors can reduce performance but not increase performance — Hygiene could cause illness but not fitness. Later on Herzberg began to use the term Maintenance as an alternative to Hygiene. It means the same thing — a working environment needs to be MAINTAINED at a reasonable standard to prevent dissatisfaction.

Personally, I prefer the term MAINTENANCE and I shall use it in this text. If you prefer HYGIENE then cross out my word and write in yours.

Now let's continue by looking at the MAINTENANCE factors and the MOTIVATORS in some detail.

## 2.2. Maintenance Factors

These are the factors which Herzberg found have the power to cause Dissatisfaction only. They do not lead to Satisfaction.

**THE FUNCTION OF MAINTENANCE FACTORS
IS TO ALLOW THE MOTIVATORS TO WORK**

— only the Motivators can cause Satisfaction.

Before looking at these Maintenance factors in a little detail let me stress that I don't expect you to memorise them. Just try to understand that these are all examples of factors in the work environment 'OUTSIDE' THE ACTUAL JOB ITSELF.

Now to the Maintenance factors:

*Company Policy and Administration* — the overall operation of the organisation — how it is managed and organised. The quality of communications would fall into this category.

*Supervision* — the social and technical ability of the supervisor. Factors under this category include: the supervisor's fairness in allocated work, knowledge of the job and the helpfulness that the supervisor gives to each member of the workteam.

*Working Conditions* — all aspects related to the physical conditions of the job, the amount of work, the facilities for performing it and the general appearance of the workplace.

*Interpersonal Relations* — the quality of the relationships between the supervisor and the workteam and between members of the workteam themselves.

*Salary* — covers all forms of monetary reward — basic pay, bonuses, shift and overtime rates.

*Status* — is the regard the organisation has for its members — sometimes shown by certain extras over and above pay. Examples include having a personal office, having a secretary, driving a company car and using the management canteen.

*Job Security* — the actual security of tenure rather than feelings of security. It includes items like fixed term contracts, lay-off agreements and redundancy procedures.

# SELF CHECK 8

TIME GUIDE 5 MINUTES

Why should a supervisor be concerned with keeping up adequate levels of these maintenance factors at the workplace. Jot down one or two ideas:

_____

_____

_____

RESPONSE CHECKOUT

Poor standard of any Maintenance factor will cause discontent or dissatisfaction.

If MAINTENANCE is poor the MOTIVATORS CAN'T WORK and performance will suffer.

**BRIEF SUMMARY**

Let's list these MAINTENANCE factors:

SUPERVISION

WORKING CONDITIONS

INTERPERSONAL RELATIONS

COMPANY POLICY & ADMINISTRATION

SALARY

STATUS

JOB SECURITY

PART B

THE IMPORTANCE OF THESE FACTORS IS THEIR POWER TO CAUSE DISSATISFACTION IF THEY ARE NOT OF AN ADEQUATE STANDARD

Once they are of an adequate standard then the Motivators can come into play to improve work performance — something that the Maintenance factors cannot do.

## 2.3. The Motivating Factors

Herzberg uses this term to describe those factors, arising directly from the job, which have the power to create satisfaction.

**THEY ARE EFFECTIVE IN MOTIVATING PEOPLE AT WORK TO GREATER PERFORMANCE AND PRODUCTIVITY.**

Before considering each of these Motivating factors in turn let me once again stress that I don't expect you to memorise them all. Just try to understand that they are all examples of factors ARISING directly from the ACTUAL JOB ITSELF.

Now to the Motivators:

*Achievement* — the personal satisfaction of completing a job, solving its problems and seeing the successful results of one's own efforts.

*Recognition* — the acknowledgement for a job efficiently done. This may arise from within the individual or be acknowledged by others.

*Work Itself* — the positive effects of the job upon the person. The job may, for example, be interesting, varied, creative and challenging. However, different people may find the same job more or less motivational. What is interesting to one person may be boring to another.

*Responsibility* — the degree of control the person has over the work. The amount of control that people can exercise is, in part, influenced by their authority and the responsibility that goes with it.

*Advancement* — the opportunity to achieve promotion within the organisation. Advancement also occurs when someone is given more freedom to exercise initiative in their normal work.

*Growth* — the opportunities to gain new knowledge and develop new skills. It may be seen as the opportunity to use developed skills and abilities or to realise fuller potential in the job.

# SELF CHECK 9

TIME GUIDE 5 MINUTES

Why should supervisors want to ensure that motivators are built into the jobs under their charge?

Jot down one or two ideas.

_____

_____

_____

_____

### RESPONSE CHECKOUT

Your response should include at least this one key idea:

- Because they encourage people at work to achieve higher performance and productivity.

**BRIEF SUMMARY**

Let's list these MOTIVATORS:

ACHIEVEMENT    RESPONSIBILITY
RECOGNITION    ADVANCEMENT
WORK ITSELF      GROWTH

PART B

## THE VALUE OF THESE FACTORS IS THEIR POWER TO PROVIDE JOB SATISFACTION FOR MEMBERS OF YOUR WORKTEAM.

In its turn this Job Satisfaction will be coincident with high individual performance and high productivity as a whole.

Thus far we've seen that supervisors should be concerned with:

- Building the motivators into the jobs under their charge.

- Keeping up an adequate standard of maintenance factors at the workplace.

You'll probably recall Part A, where we saw that the supervisor's job involves influencing the behaviour of the workteam using techniques of MOVEMENT and MOTIVATION.

Since 'movement' arises as a reaction to external forces, it can be achieved by applying Maintenance Factors. For example, bonus payments can be used to move people to put more effort into their work. But this increase in effort will not last long — people do 'get used to' extra money.

However because motivation involves the creation of willingness and enthusiasm within the individual, then it is much more difficult to achieve than movement. You can't 'provide' motivating factors in the same way you might the Maintenance Factors.

What you can do, however, is to build the motivators into the jobs of your workteam. This provides them with opportunities to develop the motivating forces WITHIN THEMSELVES. For example, you may change a job in an attempt to make it more interesting and rewarding for a person; but it's only when THEY FIND IT interesting and rewarding that they are likely to be motivated to higher performance. We also note that a job which is satisfying for one person may not satisfy another.

## MOTIVATION MEANS ADOPTING AN INDIVIDUAL APPROACH.

At this point it will be useful to draw together some of the main points developed in the Unit so far. These are:

- As a supervisor, your job involves you in influencing the behaviour of your workteam.

- This you can achieve by both 'moving' and 'motivating' them.

- 'Movement' leads to short term changes in behaviour, whilst 'motivation' achieves longer lasting change.

- Since 'movement' is a reaction to external forces it can be achieved directly by providing Maintenance Factors.

- People at work can be motivated by providing them with a satisfying job.

- If maintenance factors are not of an adequate standard then the Motivators can't work.

- A satisfying job is one that contains those characteristics Herzberg calls Motivators.

- A job that one person finds satisfying, another may not.

PART

# SELF CHECK 10

TIME GUIDE 5 MINUTES

Respond to each statement by writing TRUE or FALSE in the space provided.

a) According to Herzberg, the causes of satisfaction at work relate to the content and characteristics of the job itself. _____

b) Achievement, recognition, interesting work, working conditions and interpersonal relations are all examples of motivators. _____

c) According to Herzberg, the causes of dissatisfaction at work lie in the work environment. _____

d) The Maintenance Factors may be used to motivate people to achieve higher production. _____

e) Movement leads to short term changes in behaviour whilst motivation leads to longer lasting change. _____

f) A supervisor should always give priority to 'motivation' rather than 'movement'. _____

## RESPONSE CHECKOUT

a) **True** — When Herzberg analysed the results of his studies, he found that satisfactions only arise from the actual job and that dissatisfactions only arise from the conditions under which the job is done.

b) **False** — Since achievement, recognition and interesting work relate to the characteristics of the job itself they are examples of the motivators.

But working conditions and interpersonal relations relate to the job environment, and are, therefore, examples of the Maintenance Factors.

c) **True** — See a) above.

d) **False** — Although the Maintenance Factors can be used to influence behaviour, this according to Herzberg, does not lead to motivation. Motivation is caused by forces within the individual. Provision of Maintenance factors leads to Movement.

e) **True** — Because movement is caused by external forces, usually in the form of monetary rewards, it leads to short term changes in behaviour. We soon get used to extra money. If your employer doubled your wage would you work twice as hard? If so, for how long?

Motivation leads to longer term changes in behaviour because the people derive satisfaction from DOING the job — Motivation to work will last as long as the job does.

PART

f) False    The priority supervisors can give to 'motivating' will depend upon their work circumstances. For example on a car assembly line the most common approach is to use 'movement'.

However the total costs of movement may be too high when we include all cost e.g. absenteeism, lateness etc. By emphasising motivation the total costs may fall and production may increase.

Thus far, we have relied heavily on the work of Herzberg in our attempts to understand the causes of satisfaction at work. If we accept his ideas, then it would seem that the best way for supervisors to motivate workteams is to build the motivators into the work.

Before we discuss how you might go about doing this, we should acknowledge that some criticism has been made of Herzberg's theories.

## 2.4. Criticisms of Herzberg's Two-factor Theory

REFERENCE 6
page 65

In the book 'Behavioural Science for Managers' it is argued that, although Herzberg's ideas "have had a considerable impact upon practising managers", they have also attracted criticism. This criticism focuses on the methods Herzberg used to carry out his studies and on the conclusions he drew from them.

We are not as concerned with his methods as we are with his conclusions — so let's explore this aspect.

Herzberg points to a direct relationship between job satisfaction and productivity. He argues that by building the MOTIVATORS into the job, people at work will experience JOB SATISFACTION and, as a consequence, will achieve HIGH PERFORMANCE.

### ACTIVITY 9    TIME GUIDE 5 MINUTES

Take a few moments to think about the following question. When you've come to some conclusion, write YES, NO or NOT SURE in the space provided.

Is a satisifed workteam a productive one? _____

If you responded YES then you agree with Herzberg. Although you might have found that satisfied people tend to be more enthusiastic than dissatisfied ones, it does not follow that ALL satisfied people work hard whilst ALL dissatisfied ones don't.

REFERENCE 7
page 66

In the book 'Human Resource Management' it is argued:

"It is possible for any degree of job satisfaction to be associated with any degree of productivity, that is, a satisfied worker may have low productivity or a dissatisfied worker may have high productivity, or vice versa."

Now I must admit that I find all this a little puzzling. It seems that a simple answer to our question in Activity 9 can't be given. My own common sense would suggest that job satisfaction and productivity go together.

However I would equally admit that it is quite possible for people to put a good deal of effort into their jobs however dissatisfying these may be. They may fear the sack, be attracted by the pay or simply find working hard the best way to pass the time.

On the other hand others, particularly skilled people, combine high job satisfaction with high productivity. Perhaps they have developed a loyalty to their craft rather than to their employer.

So returning to Activity 9, it would appear that although a satisfied workteam CAN be productive, they are not necessarily so.

**SINCE THE RELATIONSHIP BETWEEN JOB SATISFACTION AND PRODUCTIVITY IS COMPLEX THEN WE SHOULD GREET HERZBERG'S FINDINGS WITH GUARDED ENTHUSIASM.**

In Part C we look at his ideas on how jobs can be redesigned to improve JOB SATISFACTION and of course PRODUCTIVITY.

Despite the difficulty in being certain about the relationship between job satisfaction and productivity I am heartened by the following remark from 'Behavioural Science for Managers':

> "... it must not be overlooked that HERZBERG has made a considerable contribution to the study of motivation at work".

Herzberg has succeeded in convincing many managers that the job content can influence work behaviour as do the more 'traditional' factors, such as money and fringe benefits.

## SELF CHECK II     TIME GUIDE 5 MINUTES

Respond by completing each sentence with a suitable word or words.

a) The relationship between job satisfaction and productivity is more _____ than Herzberg suggests.

b) It is possible for a satisfied workteam to have _____ productivity.

c) It is possible for a dissatisfied workteam to have _____ productivity.

PART

> **RESPONSE CHECKOUT**
>
> Typical words you might use are:
>
> a)  complex; complicated; difficult
>
> b)  low OR high  ⎱ YOU SHOULD NOT BE SURPRISED THAT EITHER
> c)  high OR low  ⎰ RESPONSE IS CORRECT — you will recall "It is possible for any degree of job satisfaction to be associated with any degree of productivity".

# 3. Summary

In Part B we focused upon causes of job satisfaction.

- We found that the factors involved in producing job satisfaction are separate and distinct from the factors that lead to job dissatisfaction.

- Satisfiers arise from the content of the job itself.

- Dissatisfiers arise from the work environment.

  According to Herzberg:

- The factors which can cause job satisfaction are the Motivators.

- Those which can cause job dissatisfaction are the Maintenance factors.

- The Maintenance factors may be used to 'move' workteams to achieve high productivity.

- The Motivators can be built into the job to increase both job satisfaction and productivity.

- The relationship between job satisfaction and productivity is complex.

- It does seem that for many people at work job satisfaction does lead to high productivity.

# PART C   JOB ENRICHMENT

## 1. Introduction

In Part C we concentrate on practical problems associated with motivating through job enrichment.

1. We will explore what job enrichment means.

2. We'll see how job enrichment can be applied to a variety of jobs and discuss some of the potential problems and benefits.

3. We shall also look at some of the problems associated with introducing a job enrichment programme.

## 2. Job Enrichment

According to Herzberg, if we wish to take advantage of what job Enrichment has to offer we will need to:

**IMPROVE JOB SATISFACTION AND PRODUCTIVITY BY BUILDING MOTIVATORS INTO THE JOB.**

We learned this from Part B, now let's develop these ideas of Job Enrichment a little further.

REFERENCE 8 page 66   The book 'Job Enrichment and Employee Motivation' gives an interesting view of Job Enrichment which seems to be close to what Herzberg would advise:

> "Job enrichment seems to improve both task efficiency and human satisfaction by building into people's jobs, quite specifically, greater scope for personal ACHIEVEMENT and RECOGNITION, more CHALLENGING and RESPONSIBLE work, and more opportunity for individual ADVANCEMENT and GROWTH."

REFERENCE 7 page 66

The author of 'Human Resources Management' agrees, "a job is enriched when the employee is given greater RESPONSIBILITIES and scope to make DECISIONS and is expected to USE SKILLS he has not used before".

# SELF CHECK 12

TIME GUIDE 5 MINUTES

Underline FOUR items from the following list that could be build into a job in order to enrich it.

a) More challenge.

b) More pay.

c) Greater responsibility.

d) The opportunity to make decisions.

e) More favourable company policy.

f) Better working conditions.

g) The opportunity to learn new skills.

h) The opportunity to work with others.

RESPONSE CHECKOUT

a) More challenge.
c) Greater responsibility.
d) The opportunity to take decisions.
g) The opportunity to learn new skills.

Check out the definitions of job enrichment given earlier; you'll find these are specifically mentioned. The other items listed are not part of the job itself but features of the work environment. In Herzberg's terms they are Maintenance Factors and cannot be used to motivate performance.

## 2.1. Job Rotation and Job Enlargement

Herzberg stresses the importance of distinguishing between what job enrichment is and what it is not. Job enrichment should not be confused with two other approaches to job redesign, JOB ROTATION and JOB ENLARGEMENT.

JOB ROTATION involves switching people between a number of different jobs of RELATIVELY SIMILAR COMPLEXITY.

Although this has the advantage of increasing flexibility of production, it does not lead to motivation. A young bank employee summed up job rotation when she said:

"After I'd been at the bank a few months I became bored with my job. They introduced job rotation and now I move from one boring job to another!"

PART C

JOB ENLARGEMENT involves adding more tasks of SIMILAR COMPLEXITY to the existing job.

Once again the motivational content of the job is not improved. Applied to our bank clerk above she might have said:

> "After I'd been at the bank a few months I became bored with the FEW THINGS I had to do. They introduced Job Enlargement and now I get bored with the NUMEROUS THINGS I have to do!"

Job rotation and job enlargement BOTH FAIL TO MOTIVATE because they do not offer the opportunity for growth in the psychological sense. They don't allow any development nor use latent skills and abilities; but JOB ENRICHMENT DOES.

HERZBERG claims:

REFERENCE 2
page 65

**"JOB ENRICHMENT PROVIDES THE OPPORTUNITY FOR THE EMPLOYEE'S PSYCHOLOGICAL GROWTH."**

Let's consider how these opportunities for growth may be built into a job — a process we have called Job Enrichment.

## 2.2. Job Enrichment Strategy

This strategy involves:

1. Adding a VARIETY OF MORE COMPLEX TASKS to a job over a period of time; these tasks being designed to 'stretch' people in the sense that they will have the OPPORTUNITY to use hitherto unused skills and abilities.

2. These new tasks are presented as OPPORTUNITIES rather than demands. This offers a degree of choice as to what tasks to do and when to do them. More complex tasks can be taken on by someone as and when they feel able to cope.

This needs thinking about — such a job really would have two levels. Tasks that MUST be done and tasks that MAY be done should the person WANT to do them. This will present certain planning difficulties, but it has benefits as well.

REFERENCE 8
page 66

In the book 'Job Enrichment and Employee Motivation' the authors followed this approach when introducing job enrichment at ICI:

> "An important feature of job enrichment as applied in the ICI studies, was that the changes in people's jobs were always presented in terms of OPPORTUNITIES RATHER THAN DEMANDS. Instead of a new fixed job structure being substituted for the old, the 'boundaries' of the job were made flexible. It was always possible for the individual, in practice, to ignore the new task opportunities and to continue to do the job he had always done. The changes were 'enabling' changes, allowing for a differential response from individuals."

PART

This strategy was deliberately chosen because not everyone wants their job enriched — the original job is still there but it is contained in a broader job. The original job MUST be done, but the enriched job MAY be tackled as an optional extra.

## SELF CHECK 13

TIME GUIDE 8 MINUTES

Respond by completing each sentence with a suitable word or words.

1. Job _____ fails to motivate, because it does not allow people at work to grow in the psychological sense.

2. On the other hand, job _____ does provide opportunities for psychological growth.

3. Job Enrichment involves adding a variety of more _____ tasks to the job.

4. In Job Enrichment new tasks are available within the job as _____ rather than demands.

5. With Job Enlargement, the existing job is not replaced by a new one — the boundaries of the existing job are made more _____ .

RESPONSE CHECKOUT

Typical words you might use are:

1. rotation; enlargement

2. enrichment

3. complex; difficult; skilled

4. options; opportunities; chances

5. flexible; extended; open.

Other words with the same meaning are also suitable.

# 3. Motivation: Alternative Assumptions

Before we consider how job enrichment may be applied in practice, let's return briefly to the work of Douglas McGregor.

**ACTIVITY 10**  TIME GUIDE 5 MINUTES

Take a few moments and reflect upon the three McGregor's Theory X assumptions we chose as examples earlier. Write YES, NO or NOT SURE in the space provided.

Is job enrichment based upon the
sorts of assumptions contained
in Theory X?  _____

You may recall that we used as examples of his Theory X these three assumptions:

- The average man at work has a natural dislike for work and will avoid it if he can.

- Because of their dislike of work, most people must be controlled and threatened with punishment, to get them to work productively.

- The average man at work wishes to avoid responsibility, has relatively little ambition and wants security above all.

Earlier in this unit we saw that Theory X assumptions suggest that man must be 'moved' by stick and carrot methods — motivation not being appropriate. We now know that Job Enrichment is a method of 'MOTIVATION' not fitted to a Theory X view of man.

So what kind of man will job enrichment appeal to? McGregor gives us an answer in the form of an alternative set of assumptions to Theory X which he calls THEORY Y.

## 3.1. Theory Y Assumptions About People

REFERENCE 3
page 65

Let's repeat our earlier practice and note selected examples from Douglas McGregor's Theory Y assumptions:

- The expenditure of physical and mental effort in work is as natural as play or rest.

- Men will exercise self-direction and self-control toward achieving objectives to which they are committed.

- Average human beings learn, under proper conditions, not only to accept but to seek responsibility.

EXTENSION 4
page 64

It is important to appreciate that McGregor, in his Theory X–Theory Y research is not suggesting that one set of assumptions is particularly more accurate than another. He is, however, telling us:

PART

**ASSUMPTIONS WE MAKE ABOUT PEOPLE AT WORK WILL INFLUENCE THE WAY WE TREAT THEM.**

# ACTIVITY 11

TIME GUIDE 10 MINUTES

Take a few moments and think about your workteam. List THREE assumptions you make about them as people at work. You may find this task a little difficult — you may never have asked yourself this question before. Think about how you tend to treat them — this may help.

Three assumptions I make about my workteam are:

- _____

- _____

- _____

I feel pretty sure that one or all of your assumptions are somewhere in McGregor's Theory X and Theory Y listings.

It is important to appreciate the POWER of any assumptions you make. If you assume that your people dislike work when, in reality, they seek responsibility, then attempts to 'move' them are likely to be unsuccessful and cause resentment.

Similarly, if you wrongly assume they seek to exercise and develop their skills, then once again a job enrichment programme is likely to be unsuccessful, leading to undue stress and lower productivity.

So, it's important that you really know the characteristics of your people and what they seek from work.

**MAKING ASSUMPTIONS IS FAR TOO RISKY!**

PART C

## ACTIVITY 12

TIME GUIDE 5 MINUTES

Rather than making assumptions, how would you discover the characteristics of your people and list what they want from work? Jot down a few ideas:

_____

_____

_____

_____

_____

I don't know about you, but I would try to get to know each one of my workteam as an individual. This would involve me setting aside some time for day-to-day conversation with them. Finding out their views of work, their likes, their dislikes and their ambitions.

## ACTIVITY 13

TIME GUIDE 5 MINUTES

With motivation in mind, why is it useful for you to know in advance these characteristics of your workteam? Jot down a few ideas.

_____

_____

_____

_____

There are many advantages to be gained from getting to know your workteam, I have noted these two:
- The better you know your workteam the greater will be your chances of being able to influence their behaviour.
- The more you know about them the better equipped you will be to predict their reactions to your supervision. For example, you will be able to predict the chances of success of a job enrichment programme designed to improve their productivity.

PART C

# SELF CHECK 14

TIME GUIDE 8 MINUTES

Which of the following comments display a Theory X view of man and which a Theory Y view?

Write 'X' OR 'Y' in the space provided.

a) Man dislikes work and will avoid it wherever possible. _____

b) Man can exercise self-direction and self-control at work. _____

c) The average person seeks responsibility at work. _____

d) The average human being has relatively limited ambition and prefers to be told what to do. _____

e) Man must be controlled and threatened to get him to work. _____

f) The expenditure of physical and mental effort at work is as natural as play or rest. _____

## RESPONSE CHECKOUT

A Theory X view of man is displayed by the following comments:

    a) Man dislikes work and will avoid it wherever possible.

    d) The average human being has relatively limited ambition and prefers to be told what to do.

    e) Man must be controlled and threatened to get him to work.

A Theory Y view of man is displayed by the following comments:

    b) Man can exercise self-direction and self-control at work.

    c) The average person seeks responsibility at work.

    f) The expenditure of physical and mental effort at work is as natural as play or rest.

If you can't see why, then flick back to check out.

PART C

# 4. Job Enrichment in Practice

Having explored the nature of job enrichment and the assumptions on which it is based, let's see how it might be applied in two different work situations. In the first situation we look at an actual study and in the second we test our skills.

## 4.1. Situation 1 — The Sales Representative

REFERENCE 8　In the book 'Job Enrichment and Employee Motivation' the industrial consultants who
page 66　conducted the ICI studies wrote of their findings.

Let's begin with a summary of the changes made to the ICI jobs:

*Change 1*　Sales representatives were no longer obliged to write reports on every customer call. They were simply to pass on information which they thought useful and request action when they thought it was required.

*Change 2*　Responsibility for determining when to call on customers was placed wholly with the representatives themselves.

*Change 3*　In cases of customer complaint about product performance representatives were authorised to make an immediate settlement where this was possible of up to £100.

*Change 4*　If faulty material had been delivered, or if the customer was holding material for which he had no further use, the representative now had the complete authority to decide how best to deal with the matter. For example they could buy back the unwanted stock.

*Change 5*　Representatives were given a discretionary range of about 10 per cent on the prices of most of the products they sold.

PART

# SELF CHECK 15

TIME GUIDE 10 MINUTES

Think back to what a job Enrichment programme seeks to do. It attempts to include certain motivating factors within the job.

Refer again to this summary of the ICI job enrichment programme and, make a note of ONE motivational factor which each change introduces. For example against CHANGE 1 you could write: "exercise of judgement in decision taking".

*Change 1:* _____

*Change 2:* _____

*Change 3:* _____

*Change 4:* _____

*Change 5:* _____

PART C

> **RESPONSE CHECKOUT**
>
> Your responses may be included in the following:
>
> *Change 1* — Decision Taking; Recognition; Development of Skills etc.
>
> *Change 2* — Responsibility; Growth; Challenge etc.
>
> *Change 3* — Responsibility; Recognition; Problem Solving etc.
>
> *Change 4* — Problem Solving; Challenge; Skills Development
>
> *Change 5* — Judgement; Responsibility; Achievement
>
> Other items are also suitable to include. If you are not sure flick back into the Unit to check.

REFERENCE 8
page 66

We can now look back into the ICI study to see what the writer of this experience declared the purpose of these changes were:

> "... to build up the sales representative's job so that it became more complete in its own right. Instead of always having to refer back to headquarters, the representative now had authority to take decisions on his own. He became someone with whom the customer could really do business. Each change implied a greater responsibility; together they gave the freedom and challenge necessary for self-development."

In response to these changes sales increased by 18.6%, profit margins were raised, customer complaints were dealt with more quickly, customers felt they were dealing with responsible representatives and the job satisfaction of the salesmen improved. So for this group of people

**JOB ENRICHMENT RESULTED IN BOTH INCREASED SATISFACTION AND INCREASED PRODUCTIVITY.**

It's clear from this example, that Job Enrichment will often require additional training. In other cases however the necessary abilities are developed on the job with experience.

We've seen how job enrichment was applied in practice; let's now consider how we might introduce job enrichment in the following situation:

### 4.2. Situation 2 — The Machine Operator

PART

## ACTIVITY 14

**TIME GUIDE 10 MINUTES**

John Stanley works as a lathe operator at Filby and Gladstone Engineering. For the past six months he has operated a computer controlled machine — a job he finds somewhat boring. Briefly, the job comprises feeding the instructions, in the form of punched tape, into the machine, loading the metal bar, ensuring that the tool is adequately lubricated and keeping the machine clean. When a new batch of components is required, or when there is a fault on the machine, it is corrected by a tool setter. The machined components are tested by a quality control inspector who reports any faults to John's supervisor. If John thinks there is a problem with his machine he contacts his supervisor, who then calls in the tool setter or the maintenance engineer whichever is required.

Describe, briefly, THREE changes that could be made to enrich John's job.

- _____
- _____
- _____

---

Perhaps your three changes are included in the following:

- John could be given the authority to call in the tool setter or the maintenance engineer when he thinks fit.

  This would increase his DECISION-MAKING RESPONSIBILITY.

- He could be trained to carry out minor adjustments to his machine.
  This would induce some element of GROWTH into his job.

- He could also be trained to inspect his own work. This would enable him to detect when his machine requires adjustment or maintenance.

- Thus John will be able to use and develop ADDITIONAL SKILLS.

- John could be trained to produce the punched tape providing him with opportunities for ADVANCEMENT AND GROWTH in the area of computer-aided design.

It's clear, from this example, that Job Enrichment may often require additional training. In other cases, however, the necessary abilities are developed by on-the-job experience.

PART C

**EXTENSION 5**
**page 64**

In the Book 'Job Enrichment and Employee Motivation' a number of studies are included where job enrichment was applied to a variety of jobs.

We've seen how job enrichment may be applied in practice; let's now consider its potential at your place of work.

# 5. Job Enrichment

Obviously, in a unit of this kind I cannot deal with specific job changes that will lead to job enrichment for your workteam. It really is up to you to put what you learn from this Unit to your experience of work and knowledge of your workteam. This is the all-round expertise and knowledge that only you can develop. Therefore it's up to you, and your management colleagues, to:

**CREATE THE APPROPRIATE JOB CHANGES IN ORDER TO BENEFIT FROM JOB ENRICHMENT.**

Of course, you will wonder whether job enrichment will work for you. Read the research, it's very encouraging. Virtually all the applications show positive benefits of the process.

**HOWEVER, IT MUST BE CAREFULLY THOUGHT THROUGH AND CAREFULLY APPLIED.**

Let's look at four key questions that should concern those considering taking advantage of Job Enrichment:

- Our FIRST key question is:

  *Can the jobs of your workteam be job enriched?*

  Looking at all the evidence the answer must be YES. Recall the ICI study — this demonstrated that the basically straightforward job of a Sales Representative benefited from job enrichment.

  It would seem very likely that any job can be enriched — it often demands careful thought, BUT IT CAN BE DONE.

- Our SECOND key question is:

  *Will your workteam take up the opportunities in their enriched jobs?*

  You will be able to answer this question better than I can. Experience elsewhere tells us that not everyone wants their job enriched — but that many do.

  So you give them the option — those who want enriched jobs take up the opportunities — those who don't want them don't take up the opportunities. *It's up to them.*

PART

- Our THIRD of the key questions is:

*Will a Job Enrichment programme increase the productivity of your workteam?*

REFERENCE 8
page 66

Job enrichment is a bit like starting a car — you cannot be sure that it will work until you try it. Although there is no guarantee that job enrichment will increase productivity, the research does indicate that it is likely to create substantial cost savings. Look at what Job Enrichment did for ICI sales representatives according to the book 'Job Enrichment and Employee Motivation'.

> "The main benefit demonstrated by the studies was that, compared with previously, as good or better work was not only being done, *but being done by people at a lower level in the organisation.* It is very difficult to express such a gain in financial terms but an extremely conservative reckoning, arrived at by halving all estimated annual gains or savings, would still be over £70,000 a year. This was achieved by the 140 people involved.

REFERENCE 5
page 65

HERZBERG also demonstrated in a number of studies that job enrichment does achieve increased productivity.

Our FOURTH and last of the key questions is:

*Will job enrichment increase the job satisfaction of your workteam?*

REFERENCE 8
page 66

Although you cannot be certain, it is likely that job enrichment WILL improve job satisfaction in your workteam. Much of the research suggests that this is so. The book 'Job Enrichment and Employee Motivation' records increases in job satisfaction at ICI — although in the short term, the gains in job satisfaction were less spectacular than the gains in productivity. The most significant increases in job satisfaction came in the longer run.

To recap then, the practical research evidence points to:

- Virtually any job can be enriched in some way.

- Many people will take up the enrichment opportunities presented to them.

- Job Enrichment has the potential to reduce operation costs.

- Job Enrichment has the potential to increase job satisfaction.

# ACTIVITY 15

TIME GUIDE 5 MINUTES

If you were able to apply job enrichment to even one or two jobs on your section then note TWO potential benefits you would expect to gain:

- _____

- _____

PART C

Potential benefits are increases in productivity and in job satisfaction. Of course there are other benefits too that you may have noted: reduced costs, higher morale, improved quality of work and of working.

Essentially, Job Enrichment is achieved by giving individuals greater freedom to exert SELF-CONTROL rather than be controlled by others.

Having observed some of the benefits of job enrichment, let's look at some guidelines that will help when you set out to enrich any of the jobs at your workplace.

EXTENSION 6
page 65

*A checklist for Job Enrichment*

A job may be enriched by providing OPPORTUNITIES for growth:

- Giving someone a set of tasks which forms a COMPLETE JOB; a job that gives a sense of purpose.

- Increasing the level of RESPONSIBILITY for the job. This may involve increasing the responsibility for quantity and quality of work where this can safely be done. Where appropriate this may be extended to include responsibility for the work of others.

- Reducing the strength of control and supervision, thus giving more freedom for INDIVIDUAL INITIATIVES.

- Providing people with information on HOW WELL THEY ARE DOING their job.

- Introducing new and more complex tasks into the work, thus providing GROWTH AND CHALLENGE.

- Giving specific or specialised tasks thus enabling people to BECOME AN EXPERT in a particular activity.

Think of other ideas and add them to this checklist.

# SELF CHECK 16

TIME GUIDE 5 MINUTES

Respond to each statement by writing TRUE or FALSE in the space provided.

a) Job enrichment can lead to BOTH increased satisfaction and increased productivity.  _____

b) Some jobs cannot be sufficiently enriched.  _____

c) Job Enrichment programmes always include a specific training programme.  _____

d) Not everyone wants their job enriched.  _____

PART

> **RESPONSE CHECKOUT**
>
> a) True   You may recall that the job enrichment programme for the ICI sales representatives achieved increases in both SATISFACTION and PRODUCTIVITY.
>
> b) True   Although most jobs can be enriched, some cannot be enriched enough for any real benefits to arise. For example some assembly line jobs cannot be enriched without changing the methods of production.
>
> c) False   Although job enrichment involves making changes to a job, people may not require specific training for the enriched job. For example the ICI sales representatives were given the opportunity to make on-the-spot decisions, however they were not trained to make such decisions. On the other hand, some job enrichment programmes do require specific training, as in the case of John Stanley, the machine operator, the subject of Activity 14.
>
> d) True   Some people don't want to take on more responsibility nor to be involved in decision making — they may see this as management's job. As we've seen, some people at work are prepared to do unsatisfying jobs in return for high wages.

# 6. Introducing Job Enrichment

Herzberg identified a number of steps that might be taken when introducing Job Enrichment. Four of the more useful steps are summarised below:

*Step 1 — Select appropriate jobs*

Choose to enrich those jobs:

- where satisfaction is low;

- where MAINTENANCE factors are costly to provide;

- where the financial cost of the changes is not too high;

- where MOTIVATION will make a difference.

This last point is crucial. There is no point in attempting to get people to increase their effort unless their increased effort leads to increased productivity.

*Step 2 — Devise the appropriate job changes*

Herzberg recommends the technique of 'brainstorming'. Simply list as many changes as you can, that may enrich the job EVEN IF THEY SEEM IMPOSSIBLE TO APPLY. When you've run out of ideas, then:

- ELIMINATE those changes that involve MAINTENANCE factors rather than motivation factors;

- ELIMINATE those changes that, for some clear reason, are NOT PRACTICAL;

- ELIMINATE those changes which appear to be more like JOB ENLARGEMENT rather than Job Enrichment.

REFERENCE 5
page 65

HERZBERG also suggests that the direct involvement of the people whose jobs are to be enriched may not be helpful. He writes:

> "The job is to be changed, and it is the content that will produce the motivation, not attitudes about being involved, or the challenge inherent in setting up the job."

I'm not fully convinced about his reservations. It seems contradictory to argue that enrichment is achieved by providing people with the opportunities to use their talents in the job and at the same time, deny them the opportunity of bringing these talents to bear on what they do at work. You'll have to come to your own conclusions on this one.

*Step 3 — Present the changes as opportunities*

Earlier in this section we argued that Job Enrichment should provide a job with flexibility. The changes should be options that some people will take up but others might not. You may well recall an earlier point:

> "... an important feature of job enrichment as applied in the ICI studies was that the changes in people's jobs were always presented in terms of OPPORTUNITIES rather than DEMANDS".

*Step 4 — Measure the results of the changes*

Herzberg argues that management should set up a 'controlled experiment' in order to measure the success or otherwise of their job enrichment programmes. We may not have the time nor the resources to undertake such sophisticated trials. Nevertheless it is important that you try to establish some way of measuring the change in performance. You can then decide whether or not your job enrichment programme is successful.

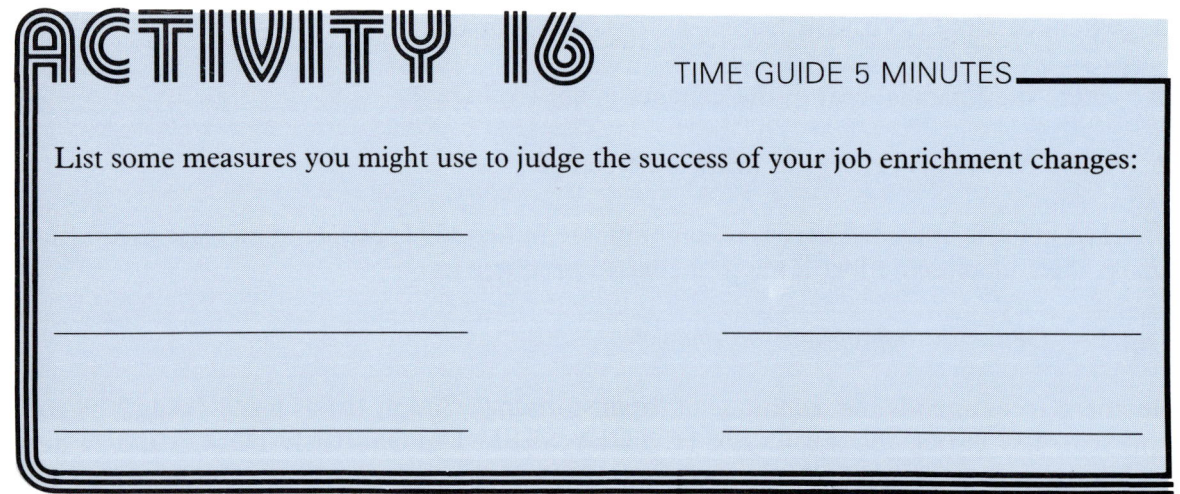

ACTIVITY 16 — TIME GUIDE 5 MINUTES

List some measures you might use to judge the success of your job enrichment changes:

PART C

The measures you've listed will very much depend on the type of work your people do. Typical measures that may be used in a variety of work situations are:

| | |
|---|---|
| Volume of production | Number of sales made |
| Number of customer complaints | Value of work produced |
| Quality of work produced | Value of sales made |
| Level of wastage and scrap | Bonus earned |
| Amount of spoiled work | Cost per unit produced |

You may have included things like higher enthusiasm, better morale, fewer grumbles. They may be less specific than the listed measures but are still useful:

Remember:

**IT'S UP TO YOU TO SELECT AND USE THE PERFORMANCE MEASURES THAT BEST SUIT YOUR WORK SITUATION.**

When introducing Job Enrichment, Herzberg asks us to be prepared for some initial drop in performance. Although the changeover to the new jobs might cause SOME reduction in efficiency, it will not last for long. THIS SHOULD NOT FRIGHTEN US OFF — it simply tells us what may be expected in the short term.

However we should appreciate that Herzberg is talking about large scale programmes. The job enrichment activities at the supervisory level are much more immediate and smaller in scale. We shouldn't expect any initial drop in performance to come from our arrangements — we can't afford it!

**SO AT THE SUPERVISORY LEVEL OUR AIMS ARE REALISTIC ENOUGH NOT TO CAUSE ANY LOSS OF PERFORMANCE, HOWEVER SLIGHT.**

PART

# SELF CHECK 17

TIME GUIDE 5 MINUTES

Complete the diagram below by inserting the following four steps in the correct sequence.

a) Present the changes as opportunities.

b) Measure the results of the changes.

c) Select the appropriate job.

d) Devise the appropriate job changes.

*Four Steps to Job Enrichment*

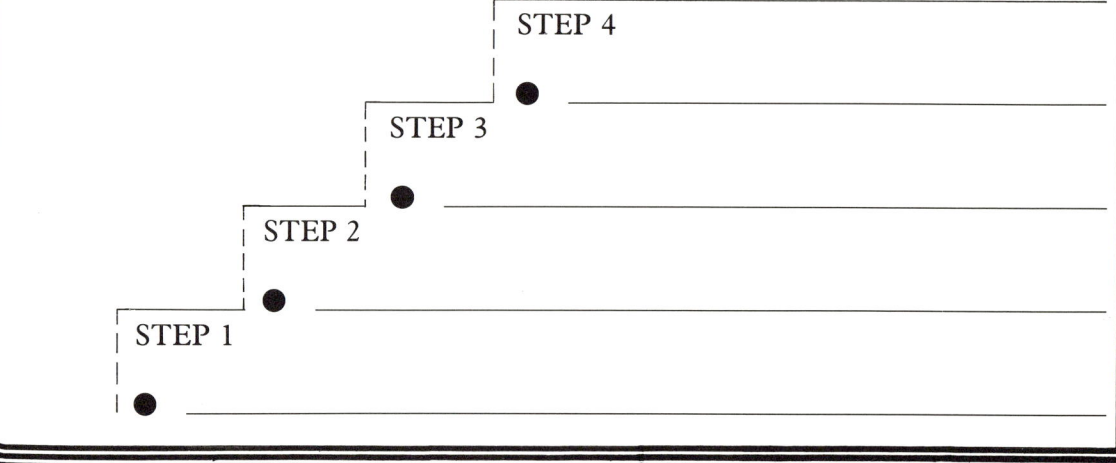

RESPONSE CHECKOUT

*Four Steps to Job Enrichment*

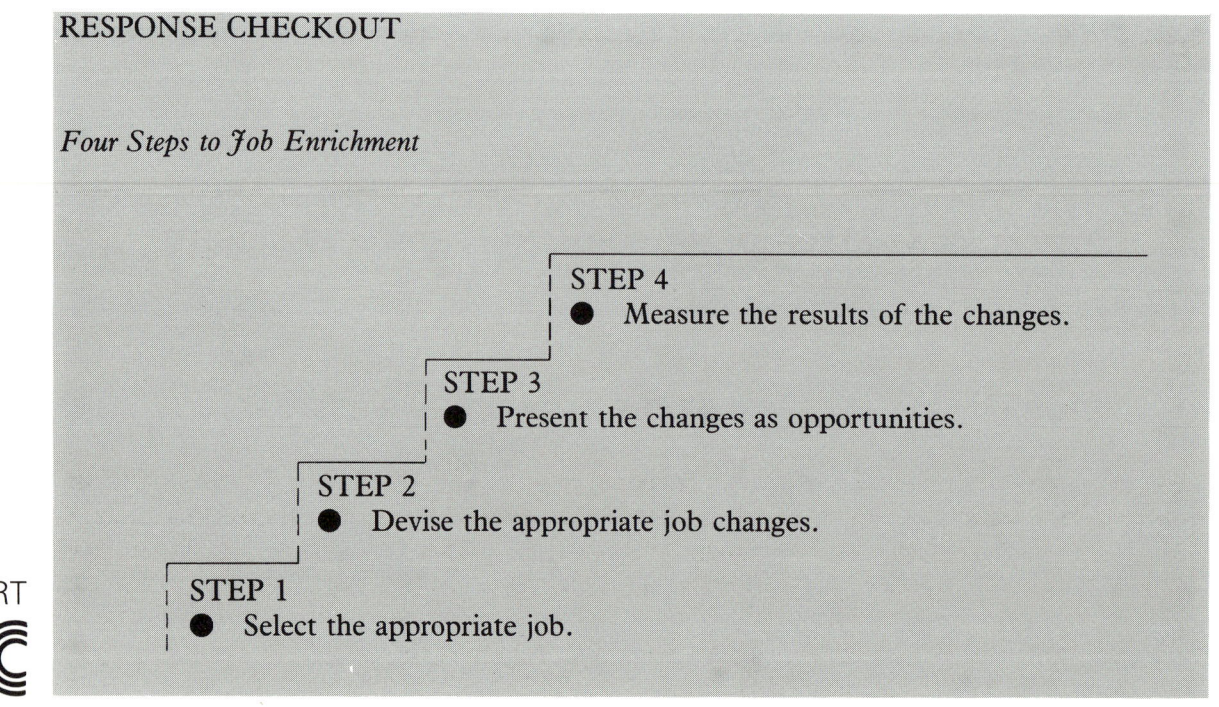

PART C

# 7. Job Enrichment and the Supervisor

Now we've looked at how job enrichment might be introduced, let's consider your part in this process.

Let's explore the part that you can play in enriching the jobs on your section.

## ACTIVITY 17 — TIME GUIDE 5 MINUTES

The table below summarises our previous Checklist for Job Enrichment. Place a tick against each item over which you have some control:

a) Give a complete set of tasks     ———

b) Increase the level of responsibility for the job     ———

c) Degree of supervision given     ———

d) Communications with workteam     ———

e) The range of tasks in the job     ———

f) Allow the person to become an expert in some specific task ———

---

I can't know which items are within your control. I just hope you were able to tick at least three of them.

Let me now turn to three areas in which most supervisors seem to have some control:

1. The range of tasks in the job.

2. Communications with workteam.

3. Degree of supervision given.

Let's discuss each of these in some detail:

**1. THE RANGE OF TASKS IN THE JOB** — the first of our three areas.

Like many supervisors you are able to exercise some control over the work of your workteam. You will often be able to allocate jobs and distribute tasks to them. In this you will be faced with the choice of doing all of your own work yourself or allow your workteam to take on some of the simpler routine duties for which you are responsible. In other words:

> in common with your management colleagues
> you face the problem of DELEGATION.

PART C

REFERENCE 9  In the book 'Supervisory Studies' it is acknowledged; "the importance of delegation lies in
page 66   ensuring that no one should be overloaded with work, otherwise efficiency will drop.
Successful delegation means that the supervisor is released from LOWER GRADE tasks, and
can spend more time on MORE IMPORTANT activities."

However routine these LOWER GRADE tasks may be to you, some of your workteam will
find them enriching at their level.

  TIME GUIDE 3 MINUTES

Take a few moments to consider the tasks you might delegate to members of your
workteam. When you have delegated in the past, did you tend to delegate the routine
tasks and keep the more interesting work for yourself?

Write YES or NO in the space provided.  _____

A YES response wouldn't be unusual! We are all human and, given the choice, would wish to
retain the interesting tasks and off-load the routine ones.

**YOU CAN ENRICH THE JOBS OF YOUR WORKTEAM BY DELEGATING
TASKS TO THEM.**

The following procedure may assist you in this process.

a)   Make a list of those tasks which should normally be performed by you (including those
     that you never get round to doing!).

b)   Examine each task for motivational content and rearrange the list in order of 'their
     potential to motivate' particular members of your workteam.

c)   Set aside those tasks that you MUST do yourself e.g. you can't delegate your responsi-
     bility for maintaining a safe place of work.

d)   Think about allocating other tasks to certain members of your workteam on the basis of
     their EXISTING AND POTENTIAL CAPABILITIES.

e)   Don't forget, as these delegated tasks are optional (opportunities not demands) you must
     be ready to do them — YOU CANNOT AVOID THE RESPONSIBILITY FOR A
     TASK BY GETTING OTHERS TO DO IT FOR YOU

f)   Give guidance and training where necessary.

g)   Follow up and check out that people are not in difficulties.

PART

2.  **COMMUNICATIONS WITH WORKTEAMS** — the second of our areas.

Earlier in the Unit we discussed the importance of giving recognition for achievements at work. Do you give such recognition? If you do, do you give it often enough and to everyone in your workteam?

## ACTIVITY 19 — TIME GUIDE 3 MINUTES

How often do you let your people know how well they are doing? — be honest! Write YES or NO in the space provided.

    MOST OF THE TIME ● _____

    ON THE ODD OCCASION ● _____

How often do you praise them when they do a good job?

    MOST OF THE TIME ● _____

    ON THE ODD OCCASION ● _____

If you don't tell them often enough how well they are doing nor praise them for doing a good job, then how are they to know? Like us they need to know — we must have something to guide our performance.

**ALL JOBS CAN BE ENRICHED BY GIVING RECOGNITION FOR ACHIEVEMENTS.**

**3. DEGREE OF SUPERVISION GIVEN** — our third and final area.

You may recall that a job can be enriched by allowing people to exercise greater control over their own work. This means giving them greater freedom to do the job their way. Of course, "their way" must be acceptable and to your standards.

## ACTIVITY 20 — TIME GUIDE 2 MINUTES

Take a few moments and think about the freedom you allow your workteam. Consider how closely you supervise them.

How frequently do you check up on your workteam? Put a tick against one of the following responses:

    MOST OF THE TIME ● _____

    SOME OF THE TIME ● _____

    LITTLE OF THE TIME ● _____

PART C

How 'closely' you supervise your people is a matter for your judgement — you need to know what's going on, but you don't want to stifle initiative and personal freedom.

**YOU ENRICH THE JOBS OF YOUR WORKTEAM BY ALLOWING THEM SOME FREEDOM TO DO THE JOB THEIR WAY.**

## ACTIVITY 21 — TIME GUIDE 2 MINUTES

I have deliberately reserved one crucial issue to the last possible moment — do you have AUTHORITY to set up job enrichment activities at your workplace? Respond YES or NO.

If you've answered YES then you are fortunate, many supervisors have little or no authority to initiate job enrichment activities.

Many others do have the chance to take SOME SMALL STEPS in Job Enrichment. I think that you will be able to think of some ways to take advantage of the benefits of doing so.

If you feel confident that you will be able to draw benefit from job enrichment then you should check that you have the authority and the confidence to move on it.

IF YOU ARE AT ALL UNSURE then check out with your manager and if necessary see what can be done to get your ideas into practice.

**IF YOU CALCULATE THAT JOB ENRICHMENT HAS EVERY CHANCE OF SUCCESS, DISCUSS IT WITH YOUR MANAGER.**

Even if you can't get the personal authority to move on job enrichment, you may be able to encourage and persuade others to do so. One way or another:

**THERE ARE THINGS YOU CAN DO TO ENRICH THE JOBS OF YOUR WORKTEAM.**

PART

# SELF CHECK 18

TIME GUIDE 10 MINUTES

Describe, briefly, THREE things that most supervisors can do to enrich the jobs of their workteam.

- _____

- _____

- _____

### RESPONSE CHECKOUT

Your ideas could be somewhere in our previous checklist which is repeated here:

- Giving someone a set of tasks which forms a COMPLETE JOB; a job that gives a sense of purpose.

- Increasing the level of RESPONSIBILITY for the job. This may involve increasing the responsibility for quantity and quality of work where this can safely be done. Where appropriate this may be extended to include responsibility for the work of others.

- Reducing the strength of control and supervision, thus giving more freedom for INDIVIDUAL INITIATIVES.

- Providing people with information on HOW WELL THEY ARE DOING in their job.

- Introducing new and more complex tasks into the work, thus providing GROWTH AND CHALLENGE.

- Giving specific or specialised tasks thus enabling people to BECOME EXPERT in a particular activity.

PART

If one of your ideas is not in this list, don't discount it. Just make sure that your idea is motivational and does provide for interest and growth, then add it to your checklist.

# 8. Summary

In Part C we concentrated on practical issues of motivating through job enrichment.

- The term job enrichment was explained and contrasted with job rotation and job enlargement.

- Some assumptions about people, on which the principles of job enrichment are based, were examined and you were encouraged to identify the assumptions you hold about the members of your workteam.

- We read of the experiences when job enrichment was applied in an industrial setting — the sales representative — the changes created more responsible and worthwhile job experiences.

- You were asked to think about some of the problems of applying job enrichment at your workplace and to assess the likely benefits; for example, increased productivity and increased job satisfaction.

- Four steps to the introduction of job enrichment were identified and some practical hints for applications were given.

- Finally, some of the things that you, the supervisor, can do to enrich your workteam's jobs, were explained, and the scope of your authority examined.

# PART D   PERFORMANCE CHECKS

Time guide
60 mins

## 1. End Check

You may now review your understanding of the Unit as a whole by completing this group of questions. DON'T GUESS THE ANSWERS — if you're not sure, flick back into the Unit and check before responding.

If your are still unsure then put a question mark against your response before proceeding.

**TRUE/FALSE**

Respond to each statement by writing TRUE or FALSE in the space provided.

1. Motivation is created by a stimulus or force within the individual. _____

2. Supervisors can motivate workteams by offering rewards for a good job and punishment for a bad job. _____

3. F W Taylor's "scientific management" appears to accept Theory Y assumptions about people. _____

4. External controls can be successful in getting people to work to the required standard. _____

5. According to Herzberg, the causes of satisfaction at work are distinct and separate from the causes of dissatisfaction. _____

6. Supervisors should give priority to MOTIVATING rather than MOVING workteams. _____

7. A satisfied person is always hard working. _____

8. Job enrichment involves adding a variety of more complex and demanding tasks to the job. _____

9. Job enrichment can lead to BOTH increased satisfaction and increased productivity. _____

**COMPLETION**

Respond by completing each sentence with a suitable word or words.

10. Supervisors may enrich jobs by allowing job holders greater _____ to do the job their way.

11. Supervisors may enrich the jobs of their workteam by _____ meaningful and interesting tasks to them.

12. The more supervisors know about their workteams, the better chance they have of adopting appropriate methods of _____ their behaviour.

13. Job enrichment provides opportunities for _____ growth.

14. Job enrichment involves adding a variety of increasingly more _____ tasks to the job.

15. According to Herzberg, the causes of satisfaction relate to the _____ of the job itself, whilst the causes of dissatisfaction relate to the job _____ .

16. "_____ management" is based upon the systematic study of work to determine the most effective methods of doing the work.

**MULTIPLE CHOICE**

Respond to each question by putting a tick against the ONE answer which is most correct.

17. When thinking of the "stick and carrot" approach, which ONE of the following is an example of the carrot?

    a) 'Abusing' an apprentice for fooling about on dangerous machinery.

    b) Promising promotion to members of workteams in return for productive work.

    c) Shouting at someone in front of their mates, for arriving late for work.

    d) Accusing someone at work of being an idiot when they have an accident.

18. Which ONE of the following is an example of a 'Theory X' type assumption about people?

    a) The average person seeks responsibility at work.

    b) The expenditure of physical and mental effort at work is as natural as rest of play.

    c) The average person must be coerced, controlled or threatened with punishment to encourage him to work.

    d) People will accept and even seek responsibility.

19. 'Scientific management' is based upon which ONE of the following:

    a) A systematic study of work to discover the most efficient methods of doing the job.

    b) A systematic study of people at work to find out what they want from work.

    c) A systematic study of reward systems to establish the best method of paying people at work.

    d) A systematic study of people to determine the most efficient methods of rewarding them.

PART

20. Which ONE of the following is an example of a maintenance factor?

   a) The opportunity to use one's skills and abilities.

   b) Increased responsibility.

   c) The chance to do interesting work.

   d) Good relationships with the supervisor.

21. A job may be enriched by which ONE of the following?

   a) Adding further similar tasks to the job.

   b) Delegating additional tasks to members of the workteam.

   c) Regularly changing the tasks done.

   d) Adding a variety of more complex tasks to the job.

22. Which ONE of the following actions is LEAST LIKELY to achieve job enrichment?

   a) Giving people at work greater freedom to do the job their way.

   b) Increasing the individual's authority and responsibility.

   c) Increasing the number of tasks in the job.

   d) Providing individuals with feedback on how well they are performing.

AUDIO TAPE SIDE 2
Time guide 35 mins

**END CHECK — Checkout**

The answers and explanations for these End Checks are on Side 2 of the Audio Tape. Have your responses with you as you play this tape. As you listen you can check out how well you have done and make notes as you proceed.

# 2. Tutor Check

Time guide 60 mins

Read the following case incident, then deal with the accompanying questions.

*Case Incident*

Bill Times worked at the head office of a travel company for ten years. Initially he found the work exciting and demanding but "the pressures of work were very high". He was earning a good salary by the travel industry standards, but was becoming increasingly frustrated with the heavy work load and the continual pressure of work.

When asked to manage a new travel agency office in Torquay, Bill jumped at the chance, seeing this as an opportunity to spend less time on administration and more time on "being a travel agent".

PART D

Bill engaged three members of staff — two counter clerks, Jenny Downs, Simon Hindmarch and a typist, Sue Yates.

Bill decided that he would organise the agency on a specialist basis as far as possible. Consequently he decided that all clients requiring an 'individual' holiday should be referred to him. He would design a package specifically for them, whilst Jenny would handle the administrative tasks associated with the holiday. Similarly, all business travel enquiries were to be handled by him.

Simon was to specialise in 'package' holidays, both in the UK and abroad, whilst Jenny was to specialise in air, rail, coach and ferry reservations and ticketing, together with car hire and independent hotel bookings. Issues related to passports, visas, foreign currency and traveller's cheques and travel insurance were dealt with by both counter clerks.

The counter staff were obliged to enter all transactions in a central filing system for easy reference. Sue was responsible for ensuring that information was correctly filed although she spent most of her time on other clerical duties and typing correspondence dictated by Bill and the two counter clerks. All letters were checked and signed by Bill.

Prizes and incentives earned by the counter clerks for the sale of special offer package tours were 'pooled' and redistributed equally between Jenny, Simon and Sue at the end of each month.

After three months of operation, Bill reviewed the performance of the agency and was not pleased with what he found. Absenteeism was increasing and the time keeping of the staff had deteriorated. A number of customers had complained about the "off hand" attitudes of the counter staff and about the quality of service in general. Some customers had even complained about the quality of the typed correspondence! Bill approached his employees and expressed his concern. He was surprised to learn that all three were not happy with their wages and Simon also added that he was "bored with the job".

Bill promised to review their wages and hinted that they would all receive a reasonable pay rise.

You only need to write ONE or TWO sentences against each question.

1. Using Herzberg's idea about money as a maintenance factor, describe the likely outcome of Bill awarding his people a substantial pay rise.

2. What will be the likely benefits of introducing job enrichment in the travel agency?

3. Describe the job changes Bill might make to enrich the jobs of the two counter clerks.

4. Advise Bill as to how he might introduce job enrichment at the travel agency.

Send to Tutor — Now get your answers to your study tutor either by post or handing it over personally. You will receive your tutor's assessment and comment back through the post as soon as can be managed.

PART D

Time guide
60 mins

# 3. Work-based Project

Earlier in the Unit we discussed a number of job changes likely to achieve job enrichment.

In this project I would like you to consider how the job of one member of your workteam might be enriched.

1. Select a job you feel would benefit from job enrichment and make a note of its title.

2. Provide a brief description of the job you've selected. If a job description exists already attach it to your project, if not, then you'll have to write one yourself.
   If you need help in this why not see your personnel or training officer or ask a management colleague.

3. Describe, briefly, the main changes you would like to see made to enrich the job. Explain how each change you've recommended would contribute towards its enrichment.

4. What would you or others have to do in order to implement your recommended changes?

I don't expect any more than ONE or TWO sentences which explains each of the ideas that you include in parts 3 and 4 above.

Send to Tutor  Now get your answers to your study tutor either by post or handing it over personally. You will receive your tutor's assessment and comments back through the post.

PART

# PART E   UNIT REVIEW

Having completed your work on this unit let's review how you feel about each of our three opening objectives. I will repeat them here and add comments.

You should be better able to:

- **"DISTINGUISH BETWEEN MOVEMENT AND MOTIVATION AND IDENTIFY THE WAY THEY ARE USED TO INFLUENCE THE BEHAVIOUR OF PEOPLE AT WORK."**

There may well be different ways of making this distinction. However, I think you should be able to base your ideas on those of Herzberg and McGregor or other people who have done a lot of work on this subject.

Now to our second objective.

You should be better able to:

- **"IDENTIFY THE CAUSES OF SATISFACTION AND DISSATISFACTION AT WORK AND DETERMINE HOW A JOB MAY BE CHANGED TO IMPROVE JOB SATISFACTION."**

Our main ideas were drawn from the work of Herzberg and we made particular reference to his TWO factor theory. We noted that the factors causing satisfaction were quite different from factors causing dissatisfaction. Referring back to our first objective you may have noticed that the factors causing DISSATISFACTION are associated with MOVEMENT and those causing SATISFACTION are associated with MOTIVATION.

You should be better able to:

- **"DEVISE AND INTRODUCE JOB CHANGES TO ENRICH THE JOBS OF THE WORKTEAM."**

We cannot talk about this objective in the same way as the others. There is only one way to check out whether you have improved your ability and that is to "use it"! In other words, the learning in this Unit really only leads to this one final objective.

You should now feel more competent and confident to be able to make the working experience of your workteam more satisfying. It is for you, WORKING WITHIN THE

LIMITS OF YOUR AUTHORITY, to discover how to utilise the ideas of job enrichment to good effect.

I hope that this work you have done was enjoyable and useful enough to encourage you to continue in your studies.

ENRICHING WORK, as we have seen, is a most important part of improving work quality and the quality of working. You will find yourself reflecting back on this work when undertaking many of the other units, none more than unit 100 NEEDS AND REWARDS, whose objectives are to help you to:

understand more of what influences people's behaviour;

list the various needs of members of the workteam;

devise ways in which a work system can be both productive for the work section and rewarding for the workteam.

PART

# PART F   APPENDICES

# 1. Extensions

I recommend that you take up as many of these extensions as you can. They will further increase your understanding and interest. You will also be able to check out a number of the ideas mentioned in the Unit. The extra time and effort will prove very worthwhile.

EXTENSION 1   Video Cassette: 'Jumping for the Jelly-beans'
B I S — Deltak Ltd.

Having dealt with Herzberg in print, you might like to see him on TV. This is a video of a lecture he gave in London and includes personal interviews in his hotel room.

EXTENSION 2   Book:        Supervisory Management
Author:      Evans D
Publisher:   Holt, Rinehart and Winston

For a brief but useful account of scientific management you might read the section headed 'F W TAYLOR (1856–1915)'.

EXTENSION 3   Book:        People and Work Organisation
Author:      Capey J G and Carr N R
Publisher:   Holt Business Texts

See section 5.8 Humanisation of Work.

The Volvo experience is referred to in this section along with other attempts to make the experience of work more human.

EXTENSION 4   You might find it interesting to read the fuller account of McGregor's Theory X — Theory Y. Read the section headed 'D McGREGOR (1901–1964)' in the book under Extension 2 above.

EXTENSION 5   Book:        Job Enrichment and Employee Motivation
Author:      Paul W J & Robertson K B
Publisher:   Gower Press

This book contains some detail of how job enrichment may be applied to a variety of jobs.

EXTENSION 6   BBC TV series 'Supervisors'
No. 4 — 'Love or Money'

It should be interesting to view this Video and see how other people actually regard their job — what they find satisfying and dissatisfying about their jobs.

## 2. References

REFERENCE 1   Book:        *Modular Programme for Supervisory Development*
                           Volume 4
              Author:      Prokopenko J and White J (Eds)
              Publisher:   International Labour Organisation, Geneva, 1981

REFERENCE 2   Book:        *The Human Side of Enterprise*
              Author:      McGregor D
              Publisher:   McGraw-Hill, New York, 1960

REFERENCE 3   Book:        *Scientific Management*
              Author:      Taylor F W
              Publisher:   Harper and Row, New York, 1947

REFERENCE 4   Book:        *The Affluent Worker: Industrial Attitudes and Behaviour*
              Author:      Goldthorpe J H, Lockwood D, Beckhofer F and Platt J
              Publisher:   Cambridge University Press, Cambridge, 1968

REFERENCE 5   Book:        *Design of Jobs*
              Editors:     Davis L E and Taylor J C
              Reading:     *'One More Time: How do you motivate employees'*
              Author:      Herzberg F
              Publisher:   Penguin Modern Management Readings

REFERENCE 6   Book:        *Behavioural Sciences for Managers*
              Author:      Boot R L, Cowling A G and Stanworth M J K
              Publisher:   Edward Arnold, London 1977

| REFERENCE 7 | Book: | *Human Resources Management* (3rd Edn.) |
| | Author: | Graham H T |
| | Publisher: | MacDonald and Evans, London 1980 |

| REFERENCE 8 | Book: | *Job Enrichment and Employee Motivation* |
| | Author: | Paul W J and Robertson K B |
| | Publisher: | Gower Press, Epping, England 1970 |

| REFERENCE 9 | Book: | *Supervisory Studies* (4th Edn) |
| | Author: | Betts P W |
| | Publisher: | MacDonald and Evans, London 1983 |

These extensions and references can all be taken up via your Support Centre. They will either have the materials or will arrange that you have access to the materials. However it may be more convenient to check out the materials with your personnel or training people at work — they may well give you access. There are other good reasons for approaching your own people, for example they will become more aware of your interest and you can involve them in your development.

If you do wish to make use of these references then don't think that you must read them right through. Just dip into them for a slightly wider treatment of the topic raised by the Unit.

PART

# NEBSS RECOGNITION

IT IS IMPORTANT TO HAVE YOUR ACHIEVEMENT RECOGNISED

The National Examinations Board for Supervisory Studies (NEBSS) makes nationally recognised awards to supervisory managers who successfully complete its courses. If you study an appropriate selection of approved units in the Super Series and complete the NEBSS assessments successfully you can obtain NEBSS MODULAR AWARDS which lead on to the CERTIFICATE IN SUPERVISORY MANAGEMENT. Some 6,500 of these are already awarded annually to students who have been successful on their courses. They come from a wide variety of industries — production, retail, catering, DHSS, Local Government and Police, to name but a few.

WHY NOT REGISTER WITH NEBSS NOW?

All you have to do is complete the registration form in this unit and send it with your registration fee to NEBSS and we will record your details on computer. We will send you your PASSPORT to a NEBSS CERTIFICATE and details of the procedure to be followed in order to obtain NEBSS MODULAR AWARDS and the full NEBSS CERTIFICATE. We cannot answer queries arising from the Unit, but we can give information about further Units, Support Centres and NEBSS AWARDS.

Please contact:　　NEBSS OPEN LEARNING,
　　　　　　　　　76 Portland Place,
　　　　　　　　　LONDON,
　　　　　　　　　W1N 4AA

ORGANISATIONS

Organisations concerned with training in any type of industry may use this material to construct their own training courses.

Membership and Professional Bodies may wish to recognise units, or groups of units for fulfilment, or part fulfilment of the educational requirements of their qualifications.

# SUPPORT CENTRES

BEDFORD COLLEGE OF HIGHER EDUCATION (0234) 51671
BOSTON COLLEGE OF FURTHER EDUCATION (0205) 65701
BRADFORD AND ILKLEY COMMUNITY COLLEGE (0274) 753000
BRIDGEND COLLEGE OF TECHNOLOGY (0656) 55588
BRIDGWATER COLLEGE (0278) 55464
CANTERBURY COLLEGE OF TECHNOLOGY (0227) 66081
CARDIGAN COLLEGE OF FURTHER EDUCATION (0239) 612032
CARLISLE TECHNICAL COLLEGE (0228) 24464
CAULDON COLLEGE OF FURTHER EDUCATION (0782) 29561
CENTRAL MANCHESTER COLLEGE (061) 831 7791
CLYDEBANK COLLEGE (041) 952 7771
COLCHESTER INSTITUTE (0206) 570271
CREWE AND ALSAGER COLLEGE OF HIGHER EDUCATION (0270) 583661
DERBYSHIRE COLLEGE OF HIGHER EDUCATION (0332) 47181
DUNDEE COLLEGE OF COMMERCE (0382) 29151
GLENROTHES AND BUCKHAVEN TECHNICAL COLLEGE (0592) 772233
HALL GREEN TECHNICAL COLLEGE, BIRMINGHAM (021) 778 2311
HEREFORDSHIRE TECHNICAL COLLEGE (0432) 267311/6
HIGHBURY COLLEGE OF TECHNOLOGY, COSHAM (0705) 383131
HUDDERSFIELD POLYTECHNIC (0484) 22288
HUMBERSIDE COLLEGE OF HIGHER EDUCATION (0482) 41451
ISLE OF WIGHT COLLEGE OF ARTS AND TECHNOLOGY (0983) 526631
NEWCASTLE COLLEGE OF ARTS AND TECHNOLOGY (091) 273 8866
NEW COLLEGE, DURHAM (0385) 62421
NORWICH CITY COLLEGE OF FURTHER AND HIGHER EDUCATION (0603) 660011
THE PERCIVAL WHITLEY COLLEGE OF FURTHER EDUCATION, HALIFAX (0422) 58221
PLYMOUTH COLLEGE OF FURTHER EDUCATION (0752) 264746
POLYTECHNIC OF WALES, PONTYPRIDD (0443) 405133
REDDITCH COLLEGE (0527) 63607/8/9
ST. HELENS COLLEGE OF TECHNOLOGY (0744) 33766
SLOUGH COLLEGE OF HIGHER EDUCATION (0753) 34585
SOLIHULL COLLEGE OF TECHNOLOGY (021) 705 6376
SOUTHAMPTON INSTITUTE OF HIGHER EDUCATION (0703) 29381 and 28182
SOUTH TYNESIDE COLLEGE (0632) 560403
SOUTH WEST LONDON COLLEGE (01) 677 8141
STANNINGTON COLLEGE, SHEFFIELD (0742) 341691
STATE MILL CENTRE, ROCHDALE (0706) 527102
STEVENSON COLLEGE OF FURTHER EDUCATION, EDINBURGH (031) 453 6161
SWINDON COLLEGE (0793) 40131
TAMESIDE COLLEGE OF TECHNOLOGY (061) 339 8683
THURROCK TECHNICAL COLLEGE (0375) 71621
WAKEFIELD DISTRICT COLLEGE (0977) 554571
WATFORD COLLEGE (0923) 41211/6
WEST BROMWICH COLLEGE OF COMMERCE AND TECHNOLOGY (021) 556 9010
WEST NOTTINGHAMSHIRE COLLEGE OF FURTHER EDUCATION (0623) 27191
WIGAN COLLEGE OF TECHNOLOGY (0942) 494911
WORCESTER TECHNICAL COLLEGE (0905) 28383
YORK COLLEGE OF ARTS AND TECHNOLOGY (0904) 704141

# THE SUPER SERIES

**PRINCIPLES AND PRACTICE OF SUPERVISION**

100 Needs and Rewards
101 Enriching Work
102 Workteams
103 Team Leading
104 Leading Change
105 Organisation Systems
106 Supervising in the System
107 Supervising with Authority
108 Workplace Control
109 Taking Decisions

**TECHNICAL ASPECTS OF SUPERVISION**

200 Looking at Figures
201 Basic Planning
202 Using Figures
203 Work and Method Study
204 Easy Statistics
205 Quality Control
206 Plant Capability
207 Controlling Output
208 Value Engineering
209 Quality Circles
210 Computers
211 Stores Control
212 Managing Time
213 Descriptive Statistics
214 Advanced Statistics
215 Supervisors and Marketing
216 General Problem Solving

**COMMUNICATION**

300 Communicating
301 Speaking Skills
302 Writing Skills
303 Communication Systems
304 Orders and Instructions

**ECONOMIC AND FINANCIAL ASPECTS**

400 Accounting for Money
401 Control via Budgets
402 Cost Reduction
403 Wage Payment Systems
404 The National Economy

**INDUSTRIAL RELATIONS**

500 Training Plans
501 Training Sessions
502 Discipline and the Law
503 Industrial Relations
504 Health and Safety
505 Industrial Relations in Action
506 Equality at Work
507 Hiring People
508 Supervising and the Law
509 Industrial Relations' and the Law

76 PORTLAND PLACE
LONDON, W1N 4AA
TELEPHONE: 01-580 3050

REGISTRATION FORM FOR OPEN LEARNING STUDENTS

PLEASE USE CAPITAL LETTERS

| SURNAME | FORENAMES (Initials are not acceptable) | SEX | AGE | Number of Years in Supervisory capacity — if any | Name of Employer if appropriate | Type of Industry |
|---|---|---|---|---|---|---|
|  |  |  |  |  |  |  |

Address

Signed: _____

Date: _____

I enclose a cheque for £5.00 made payable to NEBSS as Registration fee for a period of 3 years.

Please send me my Passport to a NEBSS Certificate.

| For NEBSS use only |  |  |  |  | Registration No. |  |  |
|---|---|---|---|---|---|---|---|
|  |  |  |  |  |  |  |  |

 **NEBSS OPEN LEARNING**

This Voucher entitles you to a FREE CONSULTATION at any of the Support Centres listed in this Unit

Make contact with the Open Learning Tutor at the Centre and arrange a convenient time for an appointment